LAWN AERATION

Turn Hard Soil Into Cold Cash

By

Robin M. Pedrotti

Prego Press
P.O. Box 35945
San Diego CA 92193

0-9629928-5-2

Library of Congress Catalog Card Number: 91-090418

International Standard Book Number: 0-9629928-5-2

Copyright @ 1992 Robin M. Pedrotti. World rights reserved. No part of this publication, including but not limited to drawings, logos, and reproductions, may be copied or reproduced in any way without the prior agreement and written permission of the author.

DEDICATION

This book is dedicated to my parents, Laura and Larry Pedrotti, for their lifelong commitment to their five sons. Their number one goal was for each of us to complete a college education. It took them two decades to succeed -- ending with me, the last and toughest to get through college. I and all my brothers, Buzz, Bruce, Gene, & Dean, thank them for their unconditional love, their forceful but loving support, and our very memorable childhoods. I wish every individual could experience the same...

ACKNOWLEDGMENTS

I would like to thank Don Learned for his intensive work as the Senior Editor and Graphic Designer of this book. He, as much as I, has made this lawn aeration opportunity come to life. My thanks also to Trevor Copenhaver, who created the cover and the drawings used in this book. In addition, I'd like to acknowledge Tom Garvey, for his assistance with the Turf Management chapter. I'd also like to recognize Don Lilly for his many contributions and support in the preparation of this book. Truer Words, of San Diego, did a great job of last-minute proofreading. Every book is a team effort and I feel this was a superb team.

TABLE OF CONTENTS

INTRODUCTION — Chapter 1
This Business Has Never Failed To Amaze Me 1

WHAT IS AERATION? — Chapter 2
A MIRACLE DRUG 9
COMPACTION 10
AERATION 10
LAWN PROBLEMS 12
    Water Runoff 13
    Poor Drainage 14
    Suffocation 14
    Trapped Gases 15
    Thatch Buildup 15
    Soil Barriers 16
    Starvation 16
BENEFITS SUMMARY 17
ABOUT MIRACLES 18

START-UP COSTS — Chapter 3
WHAT IT'S GOING TO COST 19
WHAT YOU ARE GOING TO MAKE 22
    Full-time Outlook Per Month 23
    Part-time Outlook Per Month 24

TABLE OF CONTENTS i

EQUIPMENT   Chapter 4

- DON'T BUY CHEAP 25
- AN AERATOR 26
- A TRUCK 31
- TRAILERS 32
- WHEEL CAGE 32
- THE RAMP 33
- SPREADER 35
- AIR BLOWER 36
- OTHER ITEMS 36
- MAINTENANCE 37
- SUPPLIES 38
    - Fertilizer 38
    - Soil Conditioner 38

YOUR FIRST JOB   Chapter 5

- GETTING READY 41
- PLANNING THE DAY 42
- LOADING UP 43
- ON THE JOB 45
- SURVEYING THE SCENE 46
- AERATING 48
- FERTILIZING, ETC. 50
- GETTING YOUR MONEY 51
- MOVIN' ON 51

BIDDING THE JOB   Chapter 6

- HOW MUCH TO CHARGE 53
- SUBURBAN LAWNS 54
- ESTATE LAWNS 57
- SOIL CONDITIONER 59
- AVOIDING THE TRAPS 61
- A FINAL NOTE 63

PROMOTION — Chapter 7

- GETTING THE CUSTOMER'S ATTENTION 65
- STANDING OUT! 65
- THE CORE MESSAGE 66
- PROMOTIONAL LITERATURE 67
- THE BILL CARD 67
- FLYERS 71
- BROCHURES 74
- FLYER CONTENT 76
- DISTRIBUTION 81
  - Garden Shops 82
  - Door-to-Door 82
  - Other Possibilities 85
- TELEPHONE POLE SIGNS 86
- REFERRALS 88
  - Gardener Referrals 89
  - Garden Shop Referrals 91
  - Customer Referrals 92
- ADVERTISEMENTS 93
- TELEMARKETING 93
- WRITING ARTICLES 94
- COUNTY FAIRS 95
- OTHER IDEAS 95
- SUMMARY 96

SELLING — Chapter 8

- CONVINCING THE CUSTOMER 97
- IT'S AN ATTITUDE 97
- COMMUNICATION 98
- PROMPTNESS 99
- TELEPHONE SALES 100
  - Phone Tips 101
  - A Customer Example 102
  - Closing The Sale 103
- BUILDING VALUE 104
- DEVELOPING THE NEED 105

TABLE OF CONTENTS iii

DEVELOPING THE WANT 107
WHY PEOPLE BUY 109
SALES FROM FLYERS 109
INCREASING THE SALE 110
DOOR-TO-DOOR SALES 112
SALES FROM REFERRALS 114
SELLING REPEAT CUSTOMERS 115
THE BOTTOM LINE 118
SUMMARY 119

ADMINISTRATION   Chapter 9

A BUSINESS TO RUN HERE 121
OFFICE EQUIPMENT 122
   Telephone Answering Machine 122
   Phone Lines 123
   Cordless Phone 123
   Typewriter 124
OFFICE SUPPLIES 124
   A Logo 124
   Stationery, etc. 125
   Billing Invoices 126
   Rubber Stamps 126
   Other Supplies 127
   Bank Account 127
PHONE LISTING 128
CLIENT CARDS 129
SCHEDULING 130
RECORD KEEPING 132
   Tracking Unpaids 132
   Tax Records 133
   Tax Deductions 134
   A Tax Warning 135
SEASONAL PLANNING 135
A COMPUTER 137
YOUR START-UP KIT 138
A FINAL NOTE 139
SUMMARY 140

THE BUSINESS SIDE — Chapter 10

- GETTING STARTED 141
- LEGAL FORMATS 141
- NAMING YOUR COMPANY 142
- FICTITIOUS BUSINESS NAME 143
- YOUR ADDRESS 143
- PERMITS & LICENSES 144
- INSURANCE 144
- FINANCING 146
- SUMMARY 148

TURF MANAGEMENT — Chapter 11

- WHAT YOU NEED TO KNOW 149
- ANATOMY OF A GRASS 150
- COOL SEASON GRASSES 151
  - Tall Fescue 151
  - Dwarf Fescue 153
  - Red Fescue 154
  - Kentucky Bluegrass 154
  - Turf Ryegrass 155
  - Annual Ryegrass 156
- WARM SEASON GRASSES 156
  - Hybrid Bermuda 157
  - Common Bermuda 158
  - St. Augustine 158
  - Kakuya 159
- SOIL TYPES 160
  - Clay 160
  - Sand 161
  - Loam 161
- SOIL pH 161
- FERTILIZER COMPONENTS 162
  - Nitrogen 163
  - Phosphorus 164
  - Potassium 164
  - Magnesium 164

    Sulfur 165
    Iron 165
    Calcium 166
    Types of Fertilizers 166
SOIL CONDITIONER 167
    Gypsum 167
    Lime 168
OTHER LAWN CARE ACTIVITIES 168
    Dethatching 169
    Mowers 170
    Watering 171
    Renovation 172
WEEDS 174
INSECTS 175
DISEASES 176
SUMMARY 178
A FINAL WORD 179

APPENDIXES   Chapter 12

    APPENDIX GUIDE 181
    A ... HOMEOWNER LETTER 182
    B ... WATERING INSTRUCTIONS I 183
    C ... WATERING INSTRUCTIONS II 184
    D ... TURF TIPS 186
    E ... TURF FACTS 187
    F ... PEDROTTI START-UP KIT 188
    G ... PEDROTTI LOGO KIT 189
    H ... SOURCES 190
    I ... PUBLICATIONS 191

CHAPTER 1

INTRODUCTION

I first became aware of lawn aeration when I was eight years old. An avid golfer down the street had rented some aeration equipment and was running it back and forth over his lawn. I was puzzled. He explained what he was doing. I promptly forgot it. It didn't look like as much fun as whatever I was doing at the time.

I was not big on income opportunities when I was eight.

It came back to me just as I was entering college. By then, I *was* big on money. In high school, I'd worked afternoons and weekends mowing lawns, earning $200-$300 a week, which seemed like pretty good money. Then someone showed me a small aerator, and I thought: *Okay, worst case is, I spend $1,100 on this, do enough jobs to pay it off, and I'd own the machine.* I had the money so I bought it. I still wasn't real sure what I had here.

The day it all changed came when one of my gardening business helpers approached me. He said he knew I had an aerator. He said he'd worked for someone in the lawn aeration business and knew how to sell the service. Why didn't we give it try?

So we went out one Sunday morning, door to door. If we got a job, we told people to water their lawns and I'd come back an hour later because this particular machine worked well when the lawn was wet.

INTRODUCTION

By the end of the day, we had $526. I promised my helper 25% of the $325 in sales he made. That cost me $80. I also had $35 in fertilizer expenses. When I broke that out, I realized I had just made $400 in profits in one day. I could multiply well enough. If I took that times eight weekend days a month....

I knew I was on to something, and I've been on to that something ever since. It's called *Making Money*.

That's what this manual is about: How to make money with a lawn aeration service.

I've been at it for eight years now ... part time, full time, paying my way through college, working weekends, working summers, working evenings, supplementing my normal job paycheck, buying trucks, toys and vacations ... and it has never ceased to amaze me.

You can make $1,000 a month in extra income easily by doing this part time on weekends without disrupting your normal life.

You can make $35,000, $40,000, $50,000 a year doing it full time and only working eight months out of the year.

You can make $10,000, $15,000, $20,000 a year as an all-out summer job if you're working your way through high school or college.

And I know that's true because I've done it.

There's a couple of things to warn you about up front.

This is not one of those *Get Rich Quick* schemes that says you can make $5,000 a week sitting on your tail stuffing envelopes at home.

This is a business. It is going to cost you $6,500 to buy the tools, equipment, and supplies that it takes to start this business. Exactly what that buys and what you can expect to earn are detailed in the Start-Up Costs chapter. The thing to know now is that you can pay off your initial investment in three months. After that you get to spend a high percentage of what you bring home.

The second thing to know is that what we are talking about here is hard work -- not only the physical job of aerating but the long hours of learning all the organizational, promotional, and selling skills that it takes to create a profitable business. You will be tired at night. You will know you have earned the money you made.

If you're still not daunted, then I am going to make some assumptions about you that are the prime ingredients of success in this business:

- That you are not afraid of hard work.

- That you are serious about creating an ongoing, thriving business.

- That you want to make all the money it takes to enjoy all the things you want in life.

The market is there. Lawn aeration is rapidly becoming recognized as the latest and greatest thing in lawn care. The golf course industry is booming, and more people are realizing the benefits of the aeration that is done there routinely. They want the same thing for their lawns. This is the beginning of the heyday of lawn aeration.

And the profits in this business can be incredible.

I mentioned that this business has never failed to amaze me. Let me talk a little about how it worked for me. It may give you some clues on how it can work for you.

Remember my college aerator? Frankly, it was a pretty mediocre machine. But I was zealous. I promised customers their lawns would look fantastic. The machine didn't actually deliver. So I didn't get a lot of the repeat customers that are the gold of this business. I wasn't doing the quality work that brings those customers back year after year.

So my aeration went by the wayside. Except that whenever I needed money in college, I would go out and knock on a few doors, spend a weekend aerating, then settle back to partying, er, studying, with $600 or $700 in my pocket. (This is not exactly a hard luck story.)

Then a revolutionary thing happened in 1988, just as I was breaking out of college. Well, almost breaking out. I still needed a few classes to finish my degree. I couldn't even get a real career job without the degree. And there was a Ryan Lawnaire 28 aerator just hitting the market. I knew instinctively that here was a home-use aerator that

INTRODUCTION

would do the kind of golf-course-quality aeration I hadn't been doing before.

I bought that machine on the same premise that I bought the first. It was a bigger investment, $4,000. But again, I thought: *Well, I know this machine will do a good job. I bet I can make $1,500 a month doing this part time. Worst case is, I'll do it for three months, pay off the machine, and then I'll have it around.* I couldn't help thinking, too, about what I could buy with that $1,500 a month.

So I started aerating again. The first full week I brought in $1,500 (which is what I expected to make the whole first month). The next week I brought in another $1,500. The third week I brought in even more. Almost instinctively, I started to bring some marketing tools together, switching from door-to-door sales to a flyer program. The next thing I knew, I was spending less time selling aeration and a whole lot more time doing aeration.

I didn't know how long this would last. I started in July. I knew that was the peak of the season. It was hot out. People were thinking about their lawns. They had to water them a lot. The next thing I knew, I was still aerating in November. I made about $20,000 above expenses during that five-month period.

So when I say you can make extraordinary money in this business it's because that's what has been happening to me. The income numbers I gave you earlier are not only realistic, they're a little understated, as you'll see in the Start-Up chapter. I'm not saying you won't have to work for it. I am saying you can have whatever you want.

As histories go, I did lawn aeration full time in 1989, finished my college classes, and started my career job as a sales rep with Xerox this year. But I have to confess. I still can't resist all the fast money that comes rushing in with weekend aerating. I'm still making more money there than on the other five days of the week.

I wrote this book because lawn aeration has been extraordinarily good to me, and I want to pass that opportunity on to others. I don't plan to be doing it forever, but, as I confessed, I still can't resist the money.

Though I've done it full time, I tend to think of this as an excellent part-time opportunity. I think of firefighters with days off, young families having trouble making ends meet, or military families who could use an extra dollar. I'd feel good if a struggling family man or a kid who couldn't otherwise afford to go to college grabbed onto this and took it as far as it could go.

The universal problem, of course, is that the people who need the money the most can't envision dealing with the up-front expenses. So the Business chapter talks a little about loans and financing. You might take a look at it and see if it is of any use to you.

I don't mean to oversell it. But lawn aeration has been good to me. Over the years, it has given me furniture, trucks, toys, savings, and a college education. When I graduated from college, I went to Europe on my aeration money and, I've got to tell you, it was great.

The beautiful thing about this business is that the possibilities are endless. Full time or part time, you can do it as much or as little as you want ... bring in as much or as little money as you need ... and do it whenever you like.

If there's a down side -- and I don't consider it one -- I will mention that aeration is a three-season job. Spring, summer, and fall aerations each have their own strong selling points. Winter is the off-season. Personally, I like that. I've worked hard those other months. I love having the time off and the money to enjoy that time.

If you are wondering where this manual goes from here, let me start giving you some clues. Like any business, there are ways to do this right (big bucks) and ways to do it less right (small bucks). What I'm going to give you now are what I consider to be the keys to success in this business. And I spell that word *$UCCE$$*.

I am saying there is good money to be made here. I am also saying that the way to get it, the way to make this a growing, profitable business, is:

- *Promote heavily during the first year.* I'm recommending that during the first year you spend a significant portion of your profits to promote your business. It is an investment in your future. The more customers you have the first year -- the more

INTRODUCTION

your business name becomes recognized -- the less you are going to have to do later to bring more and more dollars.

- *Consider every customer a repeat customer.* That means doing the type of quality job that assumes you will be back the following year. Think of every customer not as a $50 job, but a $500 job over 10 years. These promotion-free customers are the ones who will make your life easy and profitable.

- *Know your product.* Be willing to invest the time to learn about lawns, grasses, and aeration. Sell not only your aeration, but your expertise in lawn care. This is the key to getting those repeat customers who don't want anyone but you doing their annual aeration.

- *Sell well.* Learn selling techniques. There is a chapter devoted to selling aeration. How good you are at selling is going to determine how big a job and how many jobs you will have every time you talk to a customer.

- *Be organized.* Do your jobs and your administration as efficiently as possible. The less time you use for your paperwork, the more time you will have to make money aerating.

In many ways, these are the basic themes of this manual. You will find them echoed over and over again in a dozen different ways.

From here, you and I are going to take a step-by-step journey through every aspect of creating a lawn aeration business that will give you all the things you know you deserve out of life. This manual has been written to tell you everything you need to know.

In subsequent chapters we will talk about:

- What is Aeration?
- Start-Up Costs (and potential profits)
- Equipment
- Your First Job
- Bidding the Job
- Promotion
- Selling

- Administration
- The Business Side
- Turf Management

This book happens to be about lawn aeration, but the information on promotional concepts, selling techniques, operating efficiently, and dealing with people will be valuable no matter what you do.

How do you know whether you want to get into this business?

I think you have to be able to visualize yourself working outdoors behind the aerator. I think it helps if you are the kind of person who would get satisfaction out of making people happy as their lawns turn green and lush. Mostly, I think you have to like spending money.

So read on and enjoy. See how it all feels to you.

INTRODUCTION

CHAPTER 2

WHAT IS AERATION?

By now, you are probably a little curious about just what aeration is, what it does, and why people are willing to pay for it.

Put simply: If there's a miracle drug for lawns, it's aeration.

Nearly every problem that grasses face -- from compaction to water runoff to bad drainage to poor fertilizer intake -- is relieved or cured by a dose of lawn aeration.

Like getting your teeth cleaned at the dentist once or twice a year, lawn aeration is one of those annual or biannual lawn maintenance activities that improves the total health of the lawn.

More and more homeowners are beginning to recognize that. Others you will have to educate. We'll talk about how in Promotion.

This chapter is a brief introduction to what aeration is -- a look at the problems that lawns face and how aeration helps. In the Turf Management chapter we will go even farther -- taking a more detailed look at grasses, soils, lawn chemicals, diseases, and other lawn care activities. These are things you need to be aware of to begin developing your role as a lawn care expert that homeowners will come to rely on.

For now, understand that when you aerate a lawn, many physical improvements will be occurring to beautify the turf. You are going to

WHAT IS AERATION?

be making people happy. You are going to be making their lawns look good. And you are going to be making a lot of money.

So let's begin with one of the most common problems lawns face.

COMPACTION

Just about everything that happens with a lawn compacts the soil.

When kids play on a lawn (called traffic), that compacts the soil. When you walk on a lawn, that compacts the soil. When you water, that compacts the soil. When it rains, that compacts the soil. When you mow the grass, that compacts the soil.

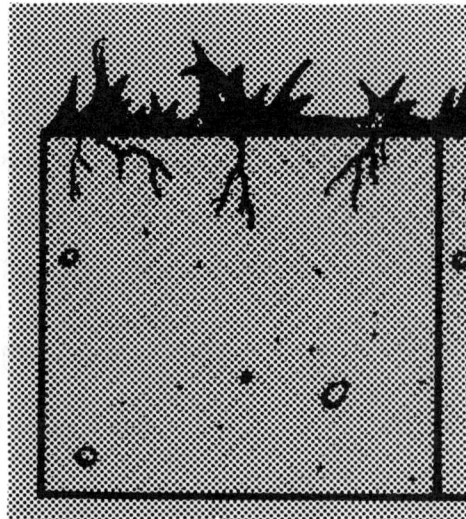

Poor Turf
Compacted Soil

There's no getting around compaction. Over time, through watering and traffic, the density of the soil will increase. Soil particles will move closer together. Large air spaces where roots can grow readily will become reduced. It's just a natural process.

What the homeowner will notice is that his ground is getting very hard. What he can't see is the struggle that grass roots are now having to penetrate that hard soil and the inability of the water to seep down to nourish the plant. What will be evident is that the grass just doesn't look as good as it once did. Dry spots will appear. It's not as healthy as it once was.

AERATION

Enter lawn aeration, specifically *core aeration*.

10 COMPACTION

Put simply, this is the process of running an aerator over a lawn surface to mechanically remove small cores of earth and grass.

By pulling out 1/2" to 3/4" cylinders of earth and grass every 2" to 3", the aerator physically removes some 10% to 15% of the soil surface.

One major impact is that this helps relieve soil compaction and makes it easier for grass roots to grow.

You can get a quick idea of how this works from the drawing on these pages. I hired an artist to do this for me and it's proven to be one of my more effective sales tools -- because, like you, a homeowner can

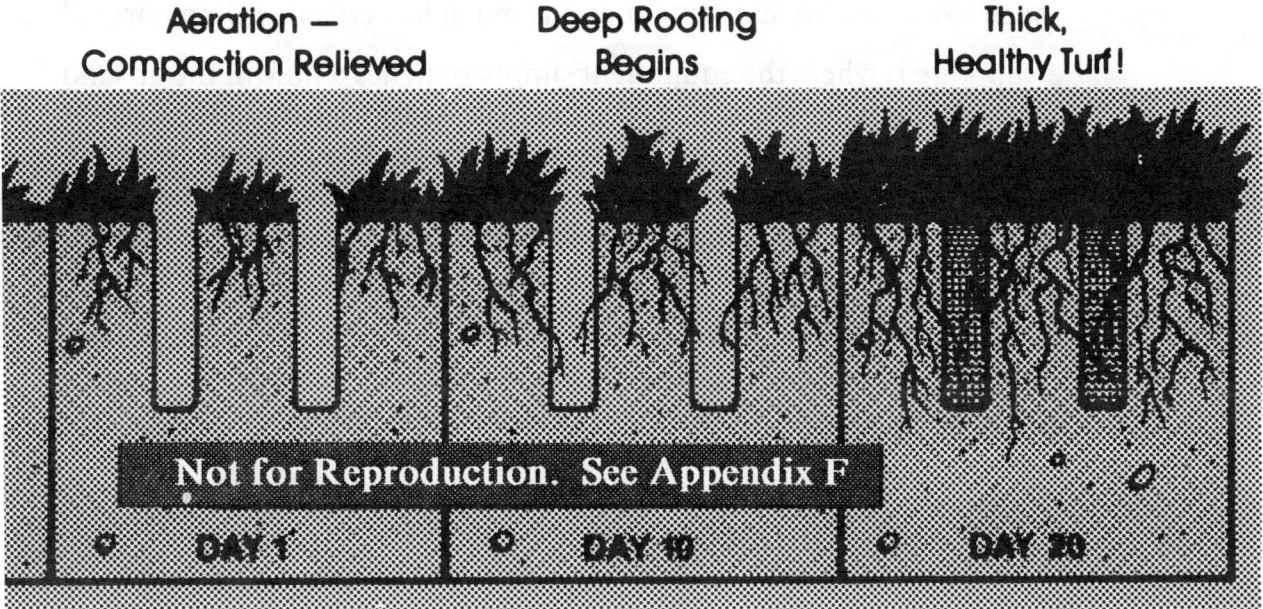

see instantly what aeration does. (I will make this drawing available to you as part of my Start-Up Kit, which we'll talk about later.)

In the drawing, you start with poor, compacted earth. Then you remove the core. Suddenly grass roots have room to grow, downward, sideward, every direction. Water can now go deeper than the roots themselves. Slowly, the holes fill in, but soil is looser. The air can penetrate it better. The root system is now deeper and healthier.

That's what the customer is paying you to provide for his lawn when he is hiring you to do an aeration job.

WHAT IS AERATION?

Technically, the word *aeration* means any kind of cultivation of the soil that improves the exchange of air between the earth and the atmosphere. Even digging a hole is aerating the soil.

But most commonly, when gardeners, golf course workers, and homeowners talk about aeration, what they mean is the process of core aeration, or *coring*. Coring is where you are taking earth out of the ground to relieve lawn problems. It is what this book is about and what I recommend you provide in an aeration service.

There's also a second type of aeration called *spiking*. It is done with much lower quality equipment and is much less effective than coring.

Spiking is where the equipment simply punches a hole in the ground without removing any soil. It does help grass roots around the 2" to 3" deep hole, but leaves the soil below that even more compacted and more of a problem. I did spiking in my early aeration days and found that it did not make happy customers. It simply doesn't provide the benefits that removing earth does.

So stick with coring. It is the kind of aeration that creates a healthier, more beautiful, more lasting lawn -- and will get you the repeat customers that produce the good profits in this business.

LAWN PROBLEMS

As grass problems go, compaction is just the tip of the iceberg.

Grasses fall prey to dozens of other obstacles. They face dozens of other difficulties they need solved in order to grow into the beautiful, luxurious turf that the guy next door would kill for.

Each of these problems represents a selling opportunity. In each case, an aeration is likely to either cure the problem or relieve it. And even if nothing is obviously wrong, you can sell aeration as preventive medicine. By contributing to the total health of the lawn, an aeration helps prevent many of these maladies from occurring in the first place.

Water Runoff

Water which runs into the street instead of soaking into the soil is no help to the grass at all. And in drought times and drought areas, it's a major social no-no. Not to mention that the homeowner is paying for water that's doing him no good.

Runoff happens for many reasons -- because of compaction, because of a slope, and sometimes for no apparent reason at all.

Sometimes the grass will just dry up and die no matter how much you water it. These are called *hot spots*, places where the lawn starts to dry out first, in the same area every time. It doesn't matter if the landscaper did a perfect job preparing the soil. These spots show up anyway. Universities have studied these hot spots to try to find out why they happen. They haven't come up with an answer.

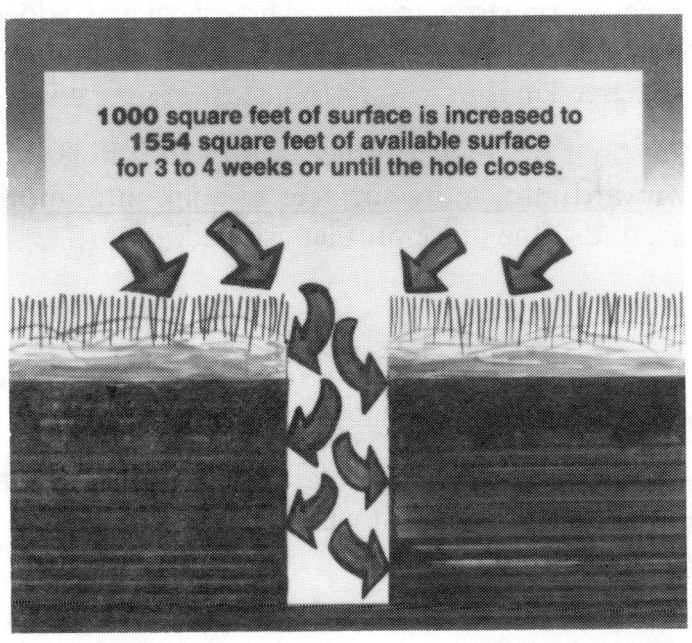

So one benefit that happens when you aerate the lawn is that you reduce the water runoff. As the adjacent picture shows, what you are doing is increasing the absorption space of a 1,000-square foot lawn by 50% to 1,500 square feet. You not only have the top of the lawn but the sides and bottom of the hole absorbing water too.

A good aeration has been known to save homeowners up to 50% on their water bill. They water less and the grass is getting even more moisture than it did before. Remember that fact: It's going to be a major selling tool when you are pushing the benefits of aeration.

LAWN PROBLEMS 13

WHAT IS AERATION?

Poor Drainage

Drainage is the ability of the water to seep downward where the grass roots need it.

When water doesn't drain well, it stays near the surface. Grass roots don't reach down for it. They stay shallow and weak. It prevents the deep rooting a lawn needs to stay healthy and vigorous.

One of the major causes of poor drainage is, again, compaction. If the soil is too hard, water may bounce off and flow elsewhere. Or it may puddle on the surface, waiting to evaporate. And even when it does get absorbed into hard soil, it may just sit in that soil without draining further. Grass roots immersed in that water often start rotting away.

Aeration relieves that poor drainage problem. It creates holes for the water to flow downward into, more surfaces to soak into, more broken earth to flow around. One more problem solved.

Suffocation

Like people, grasses need air in order to survive -- both above the ground where the blades are and below ground in the root system.

The word *aeration* stems from the idea of increased air. When doctors aerate the blood, they are flooding it with air. When you aerate the ground, you are giving the soil more air.

Homeowners don't often think about that. They understand watering because it's something they see. It runs off the lawn. It's a problem. They have to keep watering. It's a pain.

What they don't see is the air exchange. It's very important for plant roots to get oxygen. When the soil is hard, a plant doesn't get the air that it needs to grow vigorously.

When you open the soil with coring, allowing air to circulate down into the broken earth, you are helping to keep the grass plant from suffocating -- not only from too much water but from too little air.

Trapped Gases

In addition, when you have compaction, there are gases trapped in the soil that don't get released. They become poisonous because there is no way for the gas to come to the surface and escape.

So when you are aerating, not only do the plants get the air, but aeration also releases the bad gases below. It's just like your lungs taking in oxygen and letting out carbon dioxide. You don't need the carbon dioxide in your system. Grass roots don't either. Carbon dioxide and other toxic gases evolving from plant respiration and organic matter decomposition can become toxic to the root system.

Thatch Buildup

Excessive thatch buildup is another major lawn disaster. Like compaction, it is an almost universal bearer of bad tidings.

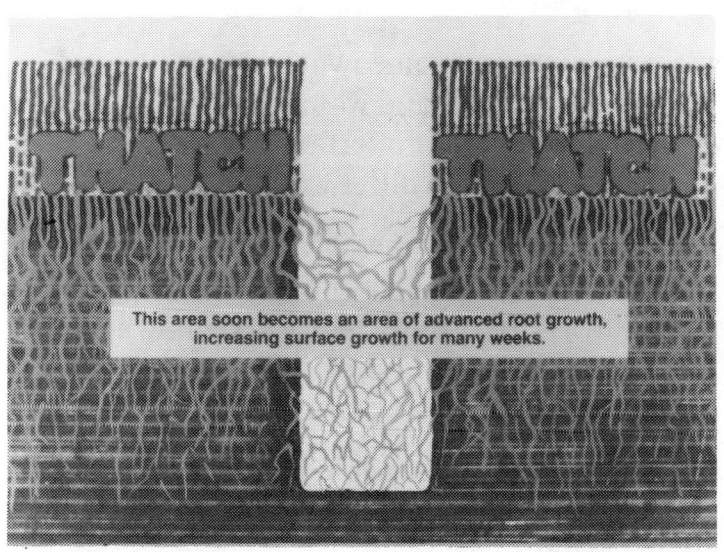

Thatch is that layer of dead and decaying plant tissue that stacks up between the soil and the green vegetation.

A thin layer is acceptable. But when it gets to be a 1/2" or more, it keeps the air, light, and water from getting to plant roots. It's another way plants get suffocated. It's also another cause of poor drainage because the water can't get through it.

Even worse, heavy thatch makes an excellent breeding ground for insects and disease organisms. If the lawn is heavily compacted or blocked with thatch, it's not going to be healthy. Like a person whose immune

WHAT IS AERATION?

system is down, the grass is going to be much more susceptible to any kind of disease or fungus attack.

Aeration relieves that problem too, because when you are taking up 15% of the soil base, you are also removing 15% of the thatch. The aeration breaks through dense thatch and opens up the soil to permit free movement of water, fertilizer, and air. That soil loosening also helps the microbacterial organisms in the soil to further break down the remaining thatch.

Even the cores left on top of the lawn after aeration have their own anti-thatch mission. It takes them about a week or so to dissolve back into the soil. As the cores break down into the thatch, soil organisms are better able to break down the dead plant layer and reduce its accumulation.

Most lawns growing on heavy clay or highly compacted soils require an annual aeration to restrict thatch accumulation.

Soil Barriers

Soil barrier problems occur when a homeowner has two or more layers of different soil and the grass roots and water can't get from one to the other. Usually referred to as a soil interface problem, it's like there's an invisible force field between the differing soils.

For example, let's say you have two inches of top soil and then a hard clay. When the grass roots and the water hit the hard clay, they stop. Thus, instead of a healthy, deep-rooted grass system, what you have is a two-inch grass carpet sitting on top of the clay. What you really want is the roots and the water to go as deeply as they can.

When you aerate, you break up that invisible barrier between the two soils. The hole itself allows roots to grow down into the second soil area and also allows the water to get there.

Starvation

Just as plants can suffocate, they can also starve. You can stand there and throw bag after bag of fertilizer on the lawn and not see it doing anything at all.

The reason is that the grass simply is getting very little of the nutrients you are throwing at it. If the soil is too compacted, if there's a heavy thatch layer, or if there's a bad soil interface, then few of those nutrient goodies are seeping down into the soil where the plant roots need them. For the grass, it's like window shopping; you can see it, but you can't play with it.

So again, by breaking up soil, by providing more surfaces for the nutrients to seep into, by allowing the fertilizer to get down to the bottom of the hole, aeration gives the grass plant a chance to have all those marvelous goodies that it needs for healthy growth.

BENEFITS SUMMARY

By this time, you should be getting a feel for what is meant by lawn aeration being a cure-all. It isn't quite. It doesn't cure everything. But it does alleviate problems in nearly all areas of lawn growth. That is why golf courses do it religiously -- usually four times a year.

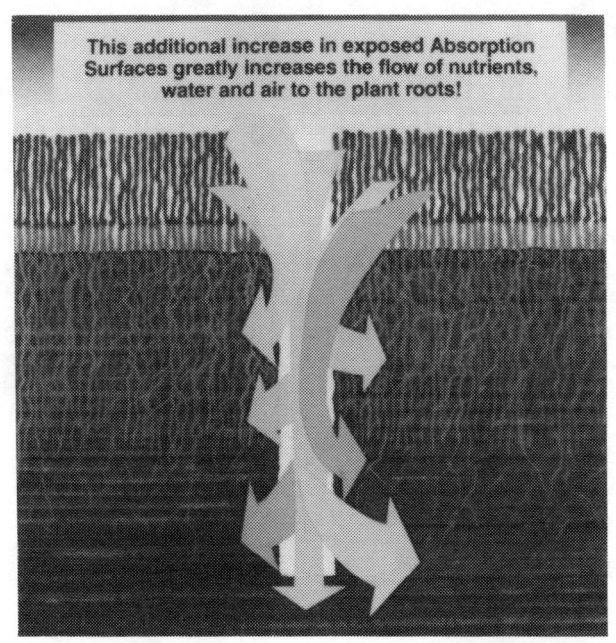

In summary, you can say that core aeration benefits a lawn in three important ways: (1) it opens the soil to permit free movement of water, fertilizer, and air; (2) it removes cores from every square foot of the lawn to relieve soil compaction and give the grass roots room to grow; (3) it removes part of the thatch and then the cores themselves break down to speed decomposition of remaining thatch.

You use these benefits in different ways in different seasons. A spring aeration provides an immediate greening. The summer market

WHAT IS AERATION?

is rescue work, as lawns dry up and brown. A fall aeration works underground, invisibly, prompting deeper rooting. You will sell each of these in season, and then take the cold winter off.

To wrap all this up in a checklist fashion, you can reel off the benefits of a lawn aeration by explaining that it:

- Reduces water runoff and puddling.
- Improves drainage.
- Improves grass rooting.
- Reduces soil compaction.
- Improves air exchange between soil and atmosphere.
- Releases harmful lawn gases.
- Enhances water intake by the plant.
- Improves fertilizer uptake and use.
- Increases tolerance to heat and drought.
- Improves resiliency and cushioning.
- Increases tolerance to diseases.

Nearly every lawn benefits from an annual aeration. Your job is to sell it twice a year. We will talk about how in the Selling chapter.

ABOUT MIRACLES

Most aeration books and brochures will caution us not to expect miracles from a single aeration. It's true. As the chapter has pointed out, there are lots of problems such as diseases and insects that an aeration will not solve.

But it's worth adding that miracles do happen -- a lot.

I've seen lawns do a complete turnaround in a matter of a week after aeration. The customers are ecstatic. Their lawn has never looked so good. They are saving tons of water. The lawns are dark and green (partly because of the soil conditioner I've developed).

So not only am I making money -- not only are you making money -- but the customers are very happy. If you like helping people, you will have your own share of rewarding experiences. Enjoy them.

CHAPTER 3

START-UP COSTS

This isn't one of those books that says: Okay, plunk down $5,000 for an aerator, I'll tell you a little about it, and you're on your own.

This book covers every aspect of starting and operating a small business -- which is what you are going to be doing. It covers equipment, supplies, promotion, sales, and administration ... right down to rubber stamps, motorcycle straps, licenses, and the kinds of grasses you are going to be burrowing holes into.

This chapter is dedicated to giving you an idea of what it actually costs to start up a lawn aeration business. In doing so, this chapter is based on several assumptions, including:

- One, if you are willing to put down the money for this book and consider the cost of initial equipment, then I'm going to assume you are serious about creating a profitable, ongoing business.

- Two, thus the approach here is not about bare minimums. It's about what it realistically costs to launch a successful business in all areas, including promotion, advertising, and administration.

- Three, the start-up analysis for starting this business does not include a pickup truck. I'm going to assume you already have one. If you don't, you will need to factor that into the start-up equation.

START-UP COSTS

We will talk about this on two levels: What I see as necessary *Start-Up* costs, plus another column on items you should consider adding *Later* as the business grows. If you have the money and are serious, you might consider going ahead and getting some of the *Later* items right away.

The following breakdown is just a summary. Details, specifics, and options of all these areas are covered in other chapters. While this list will give you an idea, you should read those other chapters thoroughly before nailing down your own start-up list.

This is what I see as necessary start-up costs:

EQUIPMENT & SUPPLIES

	START-UP	LATER
Truck		
Ryan LA-28 Aerator	$ 4,000	
Wheel Cage Holder	100	
Ramp	200	
Broom	20	
Air Blower		400
Small Spreader	70	
Professional Spreader		240
Tools / Gloves	25	
Fertilizer Bin	20	
Motorcycle Straps	20	
Irrigation Flags	5	
Earmuffs	20	
Fertilizer (5 80-lb. bags)	60	
Soil Conditioner (40 50-lb. bags)	240	
or by the truckload (480 bags)		1,400
TOTAL SUPPLIES & EQUIPMENT >	**$ 4,780**	**$ 6,580**

ADMINISTRATION

	START-UP	LATER
Fictitious Business Name	$ 60	
Post Office Box (quarterly)	20	
Permits & Licenses		
Insurance (first payment)	200	
Telephone Answering Device	100	
Second Answering Device		$ 100
Cordless Phone		230
Letterhead Stationery / Cards	240	
Three Rubber Stamps	40	
Client Cards / Box	20	
Rediform Statement Book	5	
New Bank Account Checks	25	
Scheduling Vertical File	15	
Detailed Street Map	15	
Misc. Paper clips, Supplies, etc.	25	
TOTAL ADMINISTRATIVE >	**$ 765**	**$ 1,095**

PROMOTION & ADVERTISING

	START-UP	LATER
Pedrotti Start-Up Kit	$ 79	
Paper for Bill Card	110	
Printing Promotional Literature	150	
Telephone Pole Signs	70	
Stapler Gun	30	
Sales Brochures (1200)	60	
Pedrotti Logo Package	89	
or Artist for developing own logo		350
TOTAL PROMOTION >	**$ 588**	**$ 849**

TOTAL START-UP COSTS >	**$ 6,133**	**$8,524**

START-UP COSTS

As you can see, when I say it's going to cost about $6,500 to start this business, I think that's a good round number to think in terms of.

You might be able to trim $100 or $200 here and there by not following the suggestions in other chapters. You might decide to up the ante by, say, getting an air blower right away because you realize it's going to save you time. But there are solid reasons for all the items on this list. And I've tried to be helpful. The Pedrotti Start-Up Kit and Logo Kit are designed to help you get your promotions up and running quickly. They include the formats and art work I've spent a lot of time and money developing over the years. They have been very successful. The prices and details of these are discussed in Appendixes F and G. Think seriously about every item on the list.

There's a start-up concept I heard from a gentleman who graduated from Harvard Business School called the *Card Table Theory*. That's where you start selling lemonade on a card table on the corner. Doesn't cost much. As profits come in, you expand ... to a cart, a storefront, a catering truck. Thus, the business pays for all its own growth.

Unfortunately, this is not one of those businesses.

The bad news is that nearly all your costs are going to be up-front costs. You are going to need your equipment, your supplies, and promotional literature right away in order to do the job.

The good news is that once you have all these Capital Costs out of the way, it doesn't cost much to operate on a monthly basis after that. Nearly 65% of the money you take in the first year will be pure profit, and after that the percentage will grow rapidly.

Let's take a look at that in perspective.

In your first year, full time, let's say you take $7,000 in total income each month. About 15% will cover basic operating costs -- phone, gas, truck maintenance, office supplies, insurance, and fertilizer/soil conditioner. For this year, I am strongly recommending that you spend major money, some 15-20%, on a strong promotion and advertising campaign. You have to consider this a major investment in your future; a major up-front effort to establish yourself and get your name known. That's going to cut your profits. You are going to feel like you are working your tail off and wondering why you're not getting more out of it.

But in the second year, it gets immediately better. All that up-front promotion begins to pay off. To begin with -- if you follow the recommendations in other chapters about creating satisfied customers -- about 35% of your first-year customers are likely to renew and maybe 15% will want their lawns aerated twice a year. So your promotion costs to woo new customers now drops to about 10%. Your expenses stay the same, at 15%. But now you're bringing in more revenue, $8,500 a month -- and you get to keep 75% of it.

After that, it will level off at 75% of your gross income.

In fact, by this time you can probably drop off to part time and still make as much as you did the first year because your business is well established and your customers are happy.

I'm not saying it won't take some damned hard work. I am saying it can be done.

The following chart reflects just what we are talking about here, in rounded numbers and rough percentages. The ANNUAL figure is based on being able to work eight months of the year in your climate.

FULL-TIME OUTLOOK per MONTH

Year	Income	Operations		Promotion		Net	ANNUAL	%
First	$7,000	15%	$1,050	20%	$1,400	$4,550	$36,400	65%
Second	$8,500	15%	$1,275	10%	$850	$6,375	$51,000	75%
Third	$9,000	15%	$1,350	10%	$900	$6,750	$54,000	75%

How much you can make each year depends, of course, on how long Mother Nature will let you work in your area.

In some southern parts of the country, you can do this 10 months a year -- the two extra months raising the annual intake to about $45,500 the first year, $63,750 the second and $67,500 the third.

START-UP COSTS

In more severe winter areas, you are talking about a six-month year -- $27,300 the first year, $38,250 the second, and $40,500 the third -- with time to kill doing other things between seasons.

A student, eyeing this as a three-month full-time summer job, could net $13,650 the first summer, $19,128 the second, and $20,250 the third.

If you want to look at it on a part-time basis, the numbers look like this for an eight-month season:

PART-TIME OUTLOOK per MONTH								
Year	Income	Operations		Promotion		Net	ANNUAL	%
First	$4,000	15%	$600	20%	$800	$2,600	$20,800	65%
Second	$5,000	15%	$750	10%	$500	$3,750	$30,000	75%
Third	$6,000	15%	$900	10%	$600	$4,500	$36,000	75%

At six months a year, the comparable figures become $15,600 the first year, $22,500 the second and $27,000 the third.

The possibilities are endless. The point is that once you get established some three-fourths of the money you take in will belong to you. There aren't many businesses that can make that claim.

Chapter 4

EQUIPMENT

The best advice I'm going to give you on equipment is this: **Don't buy cheap.** That's where a lot of people who start up this business make their biggest mistake.

Your equipment -- its quality, its durability, its productivity -- is what is going to keep you alive in this business. If you are going to make money, you can't afford breakdowns, you can't afford to be doing a worse job than your competitor, and you can't afford for the customer not to be happy with the job you're doing.

The major pieces of equipment you are going to need are:

- An Aerator
- A Truck
- A Ramp
- A Spreader

Major supplies you will need are:

- Fertilizer
- Soil Conditioner

The emphasis in this chapter is going to be on value rather than low price. I'm going to be recommending equipment that has staying power and that I know will do the kind of excellent job that gets you repeat customers.

EQUIPMENT

Let's begin with the aerator.

AN AERATOR

As you can see from the last chapter, this one piece of equipment represents about two-thirds of the start-up costs for going into this business. It's important to have a good one.

One aerator I recommend is the Ryan Lawnaire 28. It's the one I own. And after testing several machines and talking to others in the lawn care industry, it's the machine I keep coming back to.

To understand why that's my choice, let's look back for a moment at the evolution of aerating equipment in this country.

Ryan Lawnaire 28

In the beginning, there were just the big commercial aerators that did all the work on those beautiful golf courses.

Then in the 1960s, the same manufacturers who produced those machines began to see a potential homeowner market. They surveyed and discovered that people in the gardening industry might be willing to pay between $1,000 and $2,000 for a scaled down aerator that would handle your normal home lawn. So they produced models in that price range. They sold, and still sell, fairly well.

But there were some problems with these machines. Remember the story I told about my college-days aerator? It was in this class. It served the purpose of getting me into the market, but it did not do the type of quality aeration job that brought me the very profitable repeat customers. The truth is that machines in this price range tend to do a mediocre job.

What the home aeration industry seemed to need was a tougher machine. It needed a machine which could:

(1) Do a quality coring aeration job that will remove a significant amount of the hard soil (and not just punch holes);

(2) Be reliable enough to stand up to the abuse caused by the roots and the rocks in a typical homeowner lawn without needing frequent repairs;

(3) Be productive in the sense that it does the job fast and lets you move through each lawn and on to the next as quickly as possible;

(4) Be able to get through your standard gate easily so that you can get to back yards without a major hassle; and

(5) Be able to make turns while you are aerating so that you don't lose time having to stop and turn the machine.

In evaluating any piece of aerating equipment to start your business with, these are the criteria that the machine should be measured against. You need to talk to people in the industry about what they have heard or know about any piece of equipment in each of these areas.

Over the years, several lawn equipment manufacturers have responded to a growing demand for a good home aerator. I've watched many aerators come and go. There are a few companies out there who have created machines you should be aware of.

One is the Terracare WALK-R-IDE aerator. It's a walk-behind aerator where you can actually stand on a platform and ride with the aerator as you do the job. It's an interesting concept, and a good, well-built machine that runs about $3,000. It weighs 600 pounds, is 35" wide, and cuts a 2 3/4"-deep hole in a 3 1/2" by 4 1/4" pattern.

The key problem with the Terracare in the home aeration market is that its width and weight make it difficult to get through backyard gates. Its weight also makes it harder to load and unload from the

EQUIPMENT

truck. Compared with other machines, it is awkward in dealing with small homeowner lawn areas.

Another company in the field is Jacobsen Textron, which just bought out Classen Mfg. Inc. They have a line of aerators, of which the top two are acceptable for the home aeration market. Both of them cost about the same as the Ryan Lawnaire 28, and while their construction is strong, you'll want to compare them carefully to make sure they'll give you the reliability of a Ryan.

A business associate of mine has a Jacobsen and he complains of two problems: (1) It is very difficult to engage and disengage the tine apparatus, which makes it awkward to operate; and (2) The manufacturer suggests greasing the wheel apparatus once a day. But my associate has found that he has to stop work at least every four jobs (about three times a full day) to regrease. Otherwise, the tires will stick and the machine will become inoperable. One last problem: He says he has found that tines wear out much faster than the manufacturer suggests, and he is replacing tines frequently. That gets expensive. Still you may get a real deal on a Jacobsen and find the small adjustments during the day are offset by the Ryan's higher price tag.

One other machine you may pick up used is the Snapper aerator, which is no longer being produced. It's very small, designed like the Jacobsen, and removes cores in loose soil. It may be an aerator that can get you started in business until you can move up to a high quality machine. Or it may work out as a back-up machine.

All this talk of back-up aerators brings me back to my favorite, the Ryan Lawnaire 28. I've lived and worked with the Ryan season by season for four years now. And I'm still impressed by the quality of work it does and the abuse it can take. The LA28 runs about $4,100. I think it's worth the price tag.

I have found it to be a fantastic machine. It can take the abuse of roots and rocks. They did several improvements on the tine structure

RYAN LAWNAIRE 28

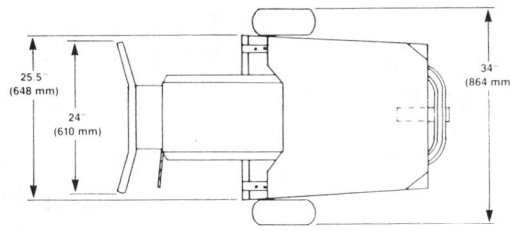

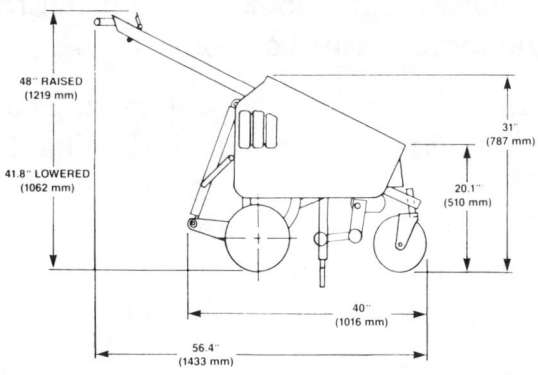

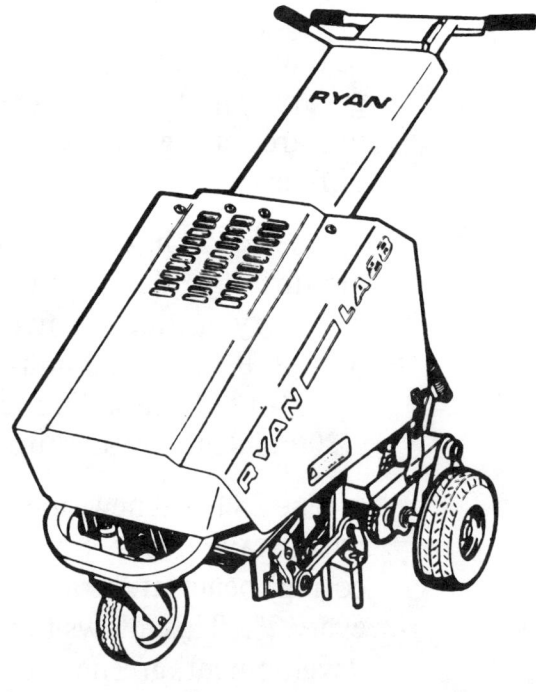

LAWNAIRE® 28 AERATOR SPECIFICATIONS
Model 544874
POWER:
Engine: OHV Wisconsin Robin, 4-cycle, single cylinder w/ cast iron sleeve; lowtone muffler; on-off switch; recoil starter
Horsepower: 7 hp. @ 3600 RPM
Bore & Stroke: 2.83" x 2.05" (72 mm x 52 mm)
Displacement: 12.92 cu. in. (211 cc)
Oil Capacity: 1 pint (.47 L)
UNIT:
Machine Type: Reciprocating self-propelled, walk-behind aerator
Drive : Wheel: A-section V-belt, #40 O-ring-sealed roller chain
Tines: B-section V-belt, #50 O-ring-sealed roller chain
Lubrication: 5 grease fittings; all sealed bearings in crankshaft and tine arm linkage. Oil bath in reversing gear boxes and grease in the differential.
Clutch: Belt tightener

Coring Depth: 2½" (63.5 mm)
Core Diameter: ¾" (19 mm)
Aerating Width: 28" (711.2 mm)
Aeration Pattern: 3½" x 5" (88.9 mm x 127 mm)
Holes per sq. ft.: Up to 12
Productivity: Up to 24,000 sq. ft. per hour
Tine Arms: 4 arms with 2 tines per arm
Tines: ¾" (19 mm) case hardened steel
Tires: Rear: 4.10/3.50-4
Front: 2.80/2.50-4
Features: Tricycle front for easy maneuverability. Rubber isolated handlebars and spring-assist lift for ease of use. Sealed, precision ball bearings at all locations in the tine arms and linkage for low maintenance and durability.
DIMENSIONS:
Weight: 400 lbs. (181 kg)
Width: 34" (864 mm)
Length: 56.4" (1433 mm)
Height: 48" (1219 mm)

AN AERATOR

EQUIPMENT

so that you get really good cores coming out of the machine. You can get about 15 to 18% of the soil base; whereas with the small equipment you are getting more like 4% or 5% of the soil base. That makes a huge difference in productivity and quality.

The LA28 has a unique tricycle design. You can aerate while you are turning. You don't have to stop -- stopping slows you down. So it's a very productive machine. It's rated as being able to do an acre an hour, but I believe a half-acre an hour is more realistic. It can also get in and out of gates. Though it's 34" wide, I've been able to get it through a 30-inch gate by angling it, because there is just one tire in the front.

The 28 has a new open-face design in the tine so that different types of soil have an easy time coming out. The tines (projections that do the coring) penetrate straight in to a depth of 2-3" and remove a 3/4" core every 2". This allows for a more professional-looking job, better root development, greener lawns, and more satisfied customers.

The one downfall of the Ryan is that there are lots of moving parts and gears. Every now and then they do need to be replaced. What I've found is that it costs about $1 a job for basic maintenance on the machine. After you do about 1,200 lawns, a fair number, you will need to renovate the machine. That costs about $2,000. I consider that a small price to pay because the machine is so reliable and it does take the abuse.

(If you are interested in this machine, I can help you purchase it. See Appendix H.)

Ryan also makes a couple of smaller machines in the Lawnaire IV and a new Lawnaire V (which has a bigger width in the back). They are okay aerators. They do a decent job and are very popular in the rental yard market because of their durability. I suppose if you

Ryan Lawnaire IV

30 AN AERATOR

are on a tight budget you could buy one of these machines. It would at least get you started in the aeration business.

But by far and away, if you are serious about going into this business and making good money, you need to buy the big aerator. In terms of quality and providing the kind of aeration that brings customers back, you are going to need a major, heavy-duty aerator such as the LA28. This is not an area where you should try to save money.

A TRUCK

The major feature of the truck needed to carry you from job to job is that it needs to have a long bed. You have lots of equipment and supplies to carry around.

If you already have a short-bed truck, then I'm not going to suggest you buy a new one. You're just going to have to use your imagination. Perhaps an overhead rack to store some of your supplies. Or any other genius trick you can come up with. The key in planning out your storage in the truck is to make it all as efficient as possible to load and unload between jobs.

If you do need to buy a truck, any of the full-sized pickups will do, such as your Ford F150 or F250, or half-ton GMC. I prefer the small trucks, like the Ranger, the Dakota, Toyota, or Nissan. (But, again, these should have a long bed.)

Some other things to think about:

- A two-wheel drive works fine. I'd stay away from the four-wheel drives. If you already have a four-wheeler, then, of course, go ahead and use it. You are going to need a longer ramp to get the equipment up into the truck. If it's a short bed you may have a real tough time getting a ramp long enough to get the equipment in the truck.

- A truck low to the ground makes it easier to load and unload equipment. Two-wheel drive trucks usually do have a low center of gravity.

- Go for high gas mileage. With my Toyota, I've gotten 20 miles per gallon (mpg) compared to 8-10 mpg in many trucks. If you

EQUIPMENT

do a lot of work during the day, that can mean a $10 gas fill-up instead of $20. Over a month, that can help make your truck payment.

TRAILERS

It is possible to start out in this business by hauling your equipment in a trailer behind your car. Not recommended, but possible. If you do, you should be thinking about getting a truck very soon.

Trailers come with some liabilities. I think they're dangerous. They can be a hazard driving down the road with all your equipment and supplies bouncing around. And they take more space to park at each job; sometimes there won't be room.

But the biggest problem is that you can't insure them, unless you have a very expensive commercial insurance policy (which we'll talk about in the Business chapter). Insurance companies will almost never cover trailers. If you get into an accident, you've got a major hassle on your hands.

If you need to, it's not impossible to start out in this business with a trailer, but think seriously about finding a truck as soon as possible. It will make your life easier.

WHEEL CAGE

If you decide to purchase a Ryan 28, the first thing you have to create is an aeration wheel cage in the front of the truck bed to handle the unique tricycle design. I called it a wheel cage because its job is to confine the aerator wheel, to lock it in place, while you are driving from place to place.

Creating this involves a rectangular bracket of heavy gage steel to park the aerator's front wheel in and two large eye-bolts to the side. Note the adjacent drawing. To get this made, you will probably have to take a copy of the drawing to a welder and have him weld the cage pieces to the truck.

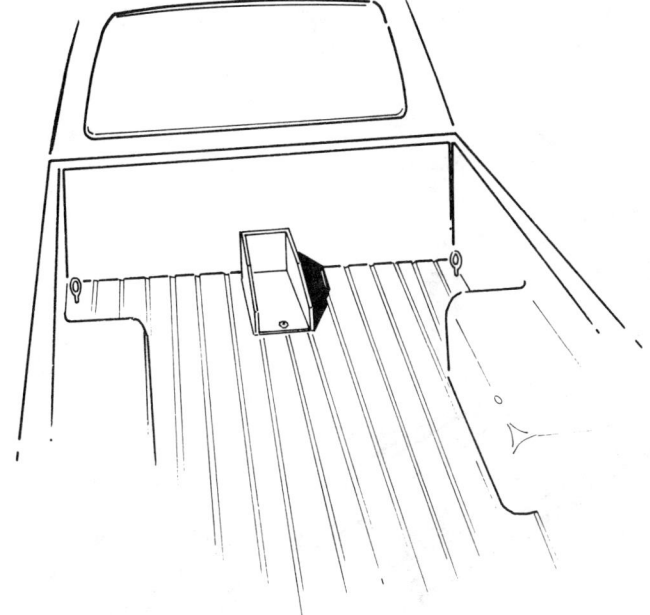

The bracket is there to hold the aerator wheel firmly -- necessary because you will find that no matter how you try to tie it down, it will always loosen up. (And remember, this is a valuable piece of equipment to you.) The eye-bolts are there so you can attach one end of a set of motorcycle straps to the bolts and the other end to the aerator handlebars. This will hold the aerator in place while you are driving and still allow easy removal of the aerator once you get where you are going.

For other aerators, the eye-bolts and motorcycle straps are still a good idea. Just make sure the aerator rides solidly. You may have to create your own version of a wheel cage. Again, it's just too valuable a piece of equipment to allow it to bounce around.

THE RAMP

Next comes the ramp. You are not going to be wanting to lift this 400-pound piece of equipment into the truck.

For this, cut down a 4'x8' sheet of one-inch plywood to fit the wheel base of the aerator. Mine measures 35"x82" to fit the Ryan. Yours should be just wide enough to fit whichever aerator you buy.

Then it's back to the welder. You are going to need a sheet frame around it and a steel lip at one end that will drop down between the tailgate and the truck bed. This anchors the ramp while you are rolling the aerator up and down. (Note the ramp drawings on page 34.) The wood and welder will probably cost around $200.

Your ramp is going to last you about two years. By then, pieces of plywood will start coming apart. It will be time to replace the wood.

EQUIPMENT

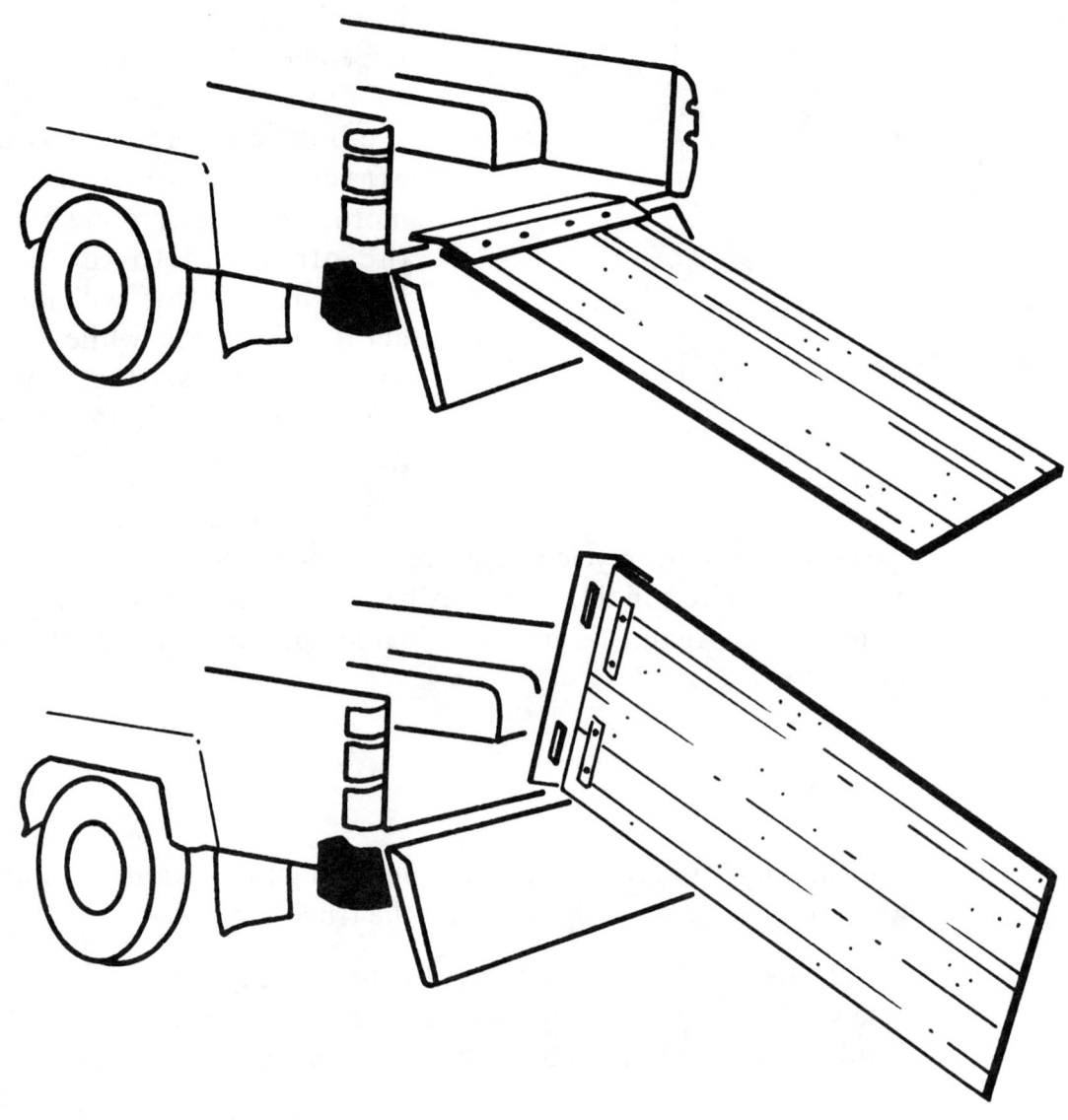

As a warning: I once tried to use 3/4-inch plywood. It collapsed on me. Luckily, neither I nor the aerator got hurt (and I'm not sure that's in right order.) So make sure your ramp is solid. You, as they say, have a lot riding on it.

SPREADER

There are many decent fertilizer spreaders around. I recommend the Cyclone model B1 made by Tru-Temper with small two-inch tires, or the B3 Pro with its sturdier four-inch tires.

This is one area of start-up costs where I can suggest that you begin with the cheaper B1 (about $70) and later upgrade to the B3 Pro (around $200) when the money starts rolling. Then you keep the B1 around as a back-up spreader.

The difference between the two is that the B3 is a much hardier machine. It will stand abuse and not wear out as quickly. The B3 has a big manifold and the wider tires. That makes a big difference. The mud from the cores will gang up on the B1, while the B3 tires make going over the lawn easier when you fertilize after the aeration. The size of tire is the same as the aerator.

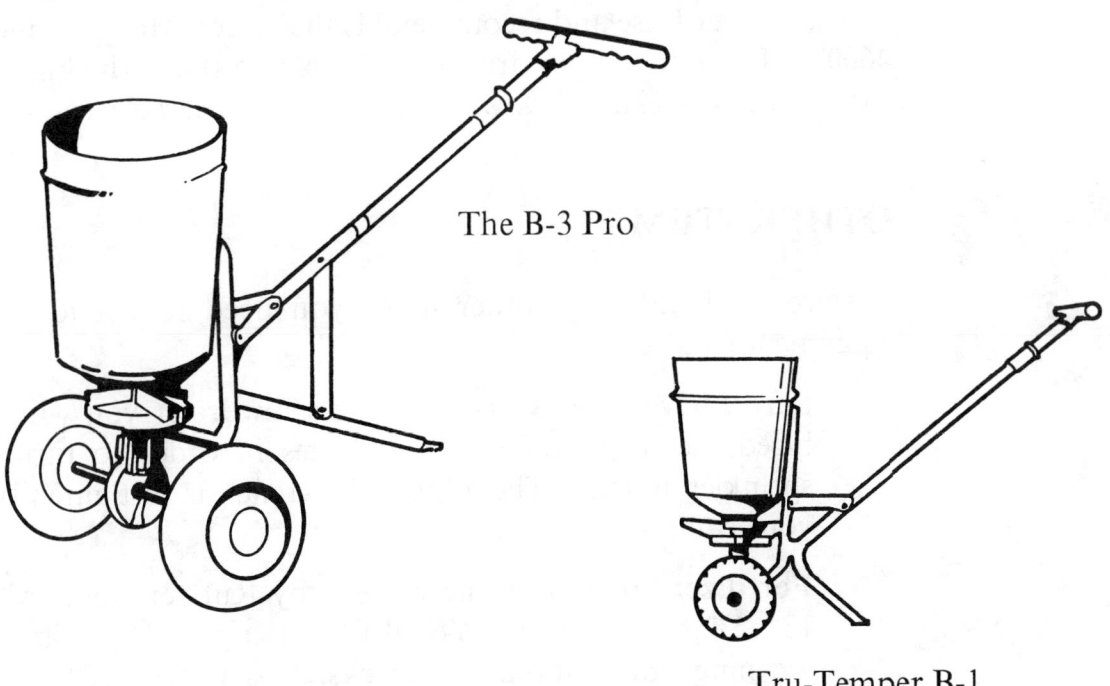

The B-3 Pro

Tru-Temper B-1

EQUIPMENT

Do stay away from plastic spreaders. They can't stand up to the abuse of many jobs.

AIR BLOWER

Aeration can be a messy job. By the time you finish, there will be cores of earth all over the lawn and sidewalks. It looks like all the neighborhood dogs just had a convention here. It's important to clear all this loose dirt, stray fertilizer, and other debris back onto the lawn. Make the area look sharp.

In your early days, you can get by with a good commercial push broom. Costs you about $20. But as the money starts rolling in, you will want to buy a good industrial-quality air blower. I say you are going to want it because sweeping up takes about 20 minutes and with an air blower you can do it in five. The blower costs about $400 though and is an investment that can be delayed.

The blower I use and recommend is the Green Machine, model LP 4600 by Echo. It's a gas driven machine, and that's the kind to look for because you can't always plug into a customer's electric service.

OTHER ITEMS

Here's a handful of other items you need to round out your equipment picture:

- **Screwdrivers & Wrench.** The screwdriver you will need to bleed the irrigation valves at times in order to turn on the sprinkler system. The adjustable wrench is to tighten bolts on your equipment.

- **Fertilizer Bin.** The one I use is by Rubbermaid. Measures 13"x23" by 16" deep. You'll fill this up with fertilizer in the morning and lift it onto the trucks. Costs about $20.

- **Leather Gloves.** Always work in a good pair of leather gloves to protect your hands. Will cost about $20.

- **Motorcycle Straps.** You need these to tie down your aerator in the truck. You can get them at any motorcycle shop for around $20.

- **Irrigation Flags.** These are very inexpensive, about 5 cents each. Buy them in bundles of 100 at any sprinkler store; they are cheaper there than at hardware stores. Besides, when you buy your first batch, it's a good time to start your relationships with the irrigation shops. It's a good opportunity to give them your business card and let them know you are in business.

- **Grease Gun.** You'll need to grease any parts of your aerator and other equipment as recommended by the manufacturer. You should do it on a daily basis. The gun you can get in an auto parts store from about $10.

- **Ear Plugs.** You'll need a set of these when you buy the blower because it's a very loud machine. Tape them to the cord with duct tape in a plastic bottle, like an empty 35mm film canister.

MAINTENANCE

Maintenance is very important in this business. It's what keeps the equipment going and the money rolling in.

As far as the aerator goes, follow the instructions of the manufacturer carefully, because the aerator is the lifeblood of your business. As a rule of thumb you want to change the oil about every 40 hours of operation. You will also need to change your tines as they wear down. The manufacturer will show you how to do that in the operating manual.

I think it's important to wash your equipment at the end of the day and, in general, just keep it clean and lubricated. Again, you need to grease the machine every day.

There are anti-rust agents you can get at the hardware store (like WD-40). You need to spray the wheels and tines occasionally. With the Ryan 28, you should also get a dry lubricant to use on the chains. You want to keep those chains in good condition because they are very expensive to replace, about $200.

EQUIPMENT

That's about it. Maintenance in this business is very low -- about 10 minutes at night cleaning and lubricating.

SUPPLIES

The two main supplies you will need in this business are fertilizer and soil conditioner. These chemical compounds help make lawns lush and green, which helps make customers happier. (Details on these lawn nutrients are provided in the Turf Management chapter.)

Fertilizer

One thing you will need most of the year is fertilizer, the nitrogen source. The nitrogen source I prefer to use is urea.

In the beginning, I suggest you buy about five 80-pound bags. That will cost about $60 and last you a week or two.

Later, you can buy in bulk quantities and save money. I usually buy it by the ton for about $250. That's 25 80-pound bags and they'll last about six months. By the ton, you'll be paying about $9.50 a bag versus $12-$13 a bag in the stores. So you save about 25%, and you don't have to constantly run to the store to pick up two or three bags.

Soil Conditioner

Your soil conditioner is going to be one of two varieties -- either a gypsum-based product on the West Coast, or a lime-based product on the East Coast.

We will discuss how to sell this in the Promotion and Selling chapters as one of the principle ways to make additional money in this business.

If you are going to use the gypsum, start with a product made by RJ SIMPLOT and marketed under the brand name *Best*. It's called Soil Buster. It's not as high in quality as a true gypsum because it's made as a byproduct and formed together with potassium. It has iron in it, which makes the grasses greener.

What gypsum does is help break up the molecular structure of the soil and to some extent leeches the salt out of the soil.

I suggest you start with a ton of this stuff -- 40 50-pound bags. It'll cost around $240. You'll be buying it for about $6-$7 a bag at your local turf distributor and selling it for about $12.50 a bag. The soil conditioner you sell to the customer by the bag.

If you are on the East Coast, the soil conditioner needs to be a lime product. The lime treatment increases the salt content and makes it easier for plants to absorb nutrients. You'll have to look around in your area and see how other people are doing their liming, because soils differ radically in different areas.

I recommend you find dealers in your area who have the new pelletized lime. That goes out in your fertilizer spreader as opposed to a drop spreader. The difference to you is that putting out the powdered lime takes about a half-hour, versus three minutes to do an 80-pound bag of the pelletized lime.

You can apply the fertilizer and soil conditioner at the same time.

If you get as good at selling soil conditioner as I'm going to encourage you to get, you can start buying this stuff by the truckload. (See Appendix H for details.)

I was fortunate to talk to someone who knew about a big manufacturer of fertilizer in Arizona. This company has a supply of natural rock gypsum that's double the strength of a powdered gypsum. It's stronger than the Soil Buster, which is its comparison product. This natural gypsum comes with iron sulfur, which helps to green up the lawn. It's about 12% sulfur.

To that, I add 4% iron. It's a special iron. There are different types of iron available and you need to make sure there's no dust in the iron. You don't want a powdered iron. *That will stain cement.* The iron is what gives the grass a darker color green.

The real advantage of this is that I'm able to reduce my cost by half from the standard gypsum product I buy from Best. And I increase the quality of the product.

Customers are happier, their lawns are greener, and I get the return business.

EQUIPMENT

CHAPTER 5

YOUR FIRST JOB

Your first job begins long before the day you actually load up your aeration equipment and head out to your first customer's lawn.

You need to have purchased your equipment and supplies, of course. Early stages of your promotional effort should be underway. You should have a few tests of your sales skills under your belt. The administrative and business details of start-up should be at least roughly organized. Details for all these are in other chapters.

By this time too, you should have a little confidence built up on running the aerator. You can do that on your lawns, family lawns, friends' lawns. Ideas for mixing early practice with early promotion by offering free aeration to people who might be able to help you in your business are offered in the Promotion chapter.

On the morning you wake up for your first job, you should also have a handful of Client Cards on the desk you are using to keep track of your aeration business. These will give you the details of the jobs you are going to do that day. (The cards are discussed in Administration.)

Earlier, you will have talked to all the customers whose yards you are going to do that day and established the following:

YOUR FIRST JOB

- When you are going to be there: Morning or Afternoon. Don't try to be more precise than that unless you are absolutely certain this will be your first customer of the day.

- What service you are going to provide: Aerate the front yard? Aerate the back yard? Add fertilizer? Add soil conditioner?

- Gotten the homeowner to agree to water his lawn the night before. The cycle is 10 minutes of watering, wait an hour to allow the water to percolate into the soil, then 10 more minutes of watering. You want the ground soft, but not soggy. Explain to the customer that aeration works best that way.

- Double-checked on the irrigation system and sprinkler heads so you know what to expect. The key thing is the depth of any irrigation lines. Professionals install these lines deep enough not to worry about. However a homeowner-installed line may be shallow enough to be hit by your aerator. A subtle way to handle that is just to ask casually about the lines and explain that you don't repair them. Mention that it's rare to hit one, but that you don't take the responsibility if they were not installed correctly.

- Asked about drains. Sprinkler heads can be found, but these little 2"-4" drains can be hidden in the grass. It's best to ask the homeowner to mark these if he or she has any.

- Checked on locked gates if you're going to do the back yard and made arrangements to have a key available.

All these details of things you've already handled should be on your Client Cards, and the fertilizer/conditioner supplies you're going to need for the day should be ready to go.

Okay. One more sip of coffee. Let's get moving.

PLANNING THE DAY

The first thing to do is grab the Client Cards for the day.

With these in hand, you want to: Get all your information packets together (Promotion chapter) and addressed for the day's jobs. Sort the cards in the order you will do the jobs. Plan it so you don't waste time traveling between customers or in traffic. Line up where you are going, from card to card. Get your invoicing ready by applying all the stamps (covered in Administration), and writing in the customer's name, job description, and the cost agreed to. This will save you time later because you are going to be doing your invoicing on the spot.

Paperclip the sorted cards together and put them in the cab of the truck. With them go your map, invoice book, pens, and a few extra blank cards just in case you pick up another job or two from neighbors along the way.

In your truck should already be a stack of brochures (covered in Promotion). These will have your business name and phone number stamped on them. You can give these out to gardeners and people who ask about aeration as you do the jobs. You should have business cards in your wallet.

LOADING UP

Okay, let's get the equipment and supplies loaded.

First, attach the ramp to the back of the truck. Start the aerator and drive it up onto the truck bed. Secure it in the wheel cage.

Put in the fertilizer container with the 30 or 40 pounds of fertilizer you're going to need for the day.

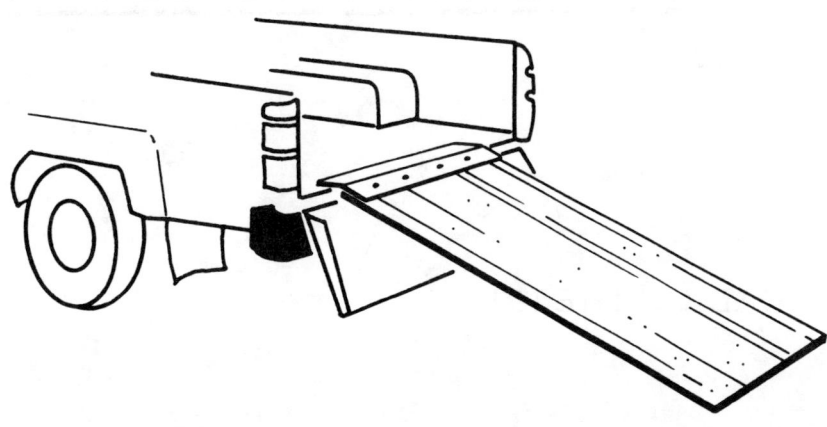

YOUR FIRST JOB

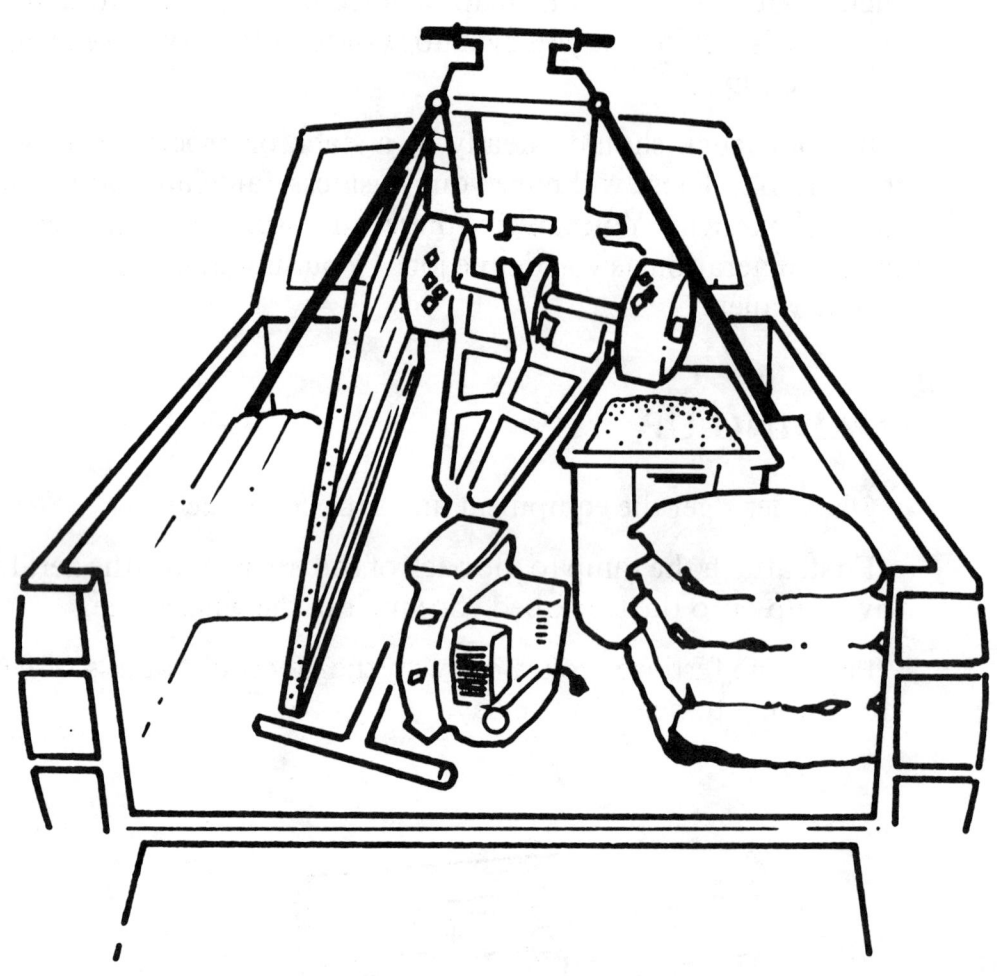

LOADING THE TRUCK

44 *LOADING UP*

Then the spreader goes in, upside down. And the air **blower, if you** have one.

Last come the bags of soil conditioner; one 50-pound bag per 1,000-1,300 square feet of lawn to be done. The soil conditioner you sell by the bag, so you already know how many bags you'll need. Either you've negotiated the number of bags with the customer, or you already know lawn sizes in that area (and how many bags it takes), or you've gotten a lawn size estimate from the customer.

With the conditioner, you may have to do a little schedule adjusting. Say, for example, you have sold 25 bags for that day and you only have room on the truck for half that. The way to handle that is to load up what you need for the morning, then come back at lunch and load the rest. If you need to shift customers from morning to afternoon to make it work, give them a quick call to let them know. My Toyota will handle about 15 bags. Normally I load about 10 in the morning and come back for more at noon, unless it's a distant job. It doesn't hurt to have extra bags for customers who change their mind about not adding it, or for an extra job you might pick up from a neighbor during the day.

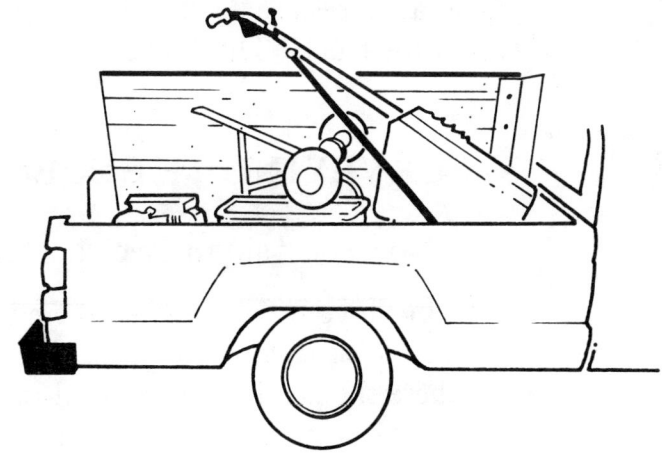

The final step is to load the ramp next to the aerator. Then you use the motorcycle straps to tie down both the ramp and aerator.

You are ready to go.

ON THE JOB

When you get to the job, don't spend much time kibitzing with customers.

Often the people aren't even home. They've already contracted with you to do the job. So I suggest you just get started; without ringing on

YOUR FIRST JOB

the doorbell and wasting time explaining what it is you are going to be doing. If you just start working, customers tend to ask fewer questions and stay out of your way. And that's what you want -- to do the job with as few interruptions as possible. That way you increase your productivity and increase your profits.

So just start unloading the truck. Throw the conditioner down next to where the ramp will be; not very far away, so that it's easy to pick up. Set the fertilizer down on the side of the truck; in the street or driveway or off to the side.

Take out the spreader and the air blower (if you have one).

The air blower you need to watch. Thieves love them. If you are going to be working in the back yard, you might put it there right away. If you're only working the front, just keep an eye on it. I've never heard of anybody getting a spreader ripped off, but air blowers and weed-eaters are hot items.

Then pull out your ramp and attach it. Undo the tie-downs on the aerator, release its dog clutch, and roll the aerator down the ramp and off the truck. That's the last step of the unloading.

SURVEYING THE SCENE

Now you want to check the lawns for any potential problems.

Grab your flags and start finding sprinkler heads. Put a flag on the outside of each head. (See illustration.) You want to know exactly where the head is and how close you can come to it with the aerator. You can turn on the sprinkler system to make sure you didn't miss any heads. If they are concealed, you may even have to do this first. The goal, of course, is to avoid breaking any heads. They cost you time and money to replace.

Check for drains. Hopefully, you've had the homeowner mark them for you, because they can be hard to find. They usually measure 2" to 4" in diameter and grass grows over them. Just look at the obvious low spots in the lawn. Drains are becoming more popular in California because the soils are so bad. Flag them, but don't worry about it too

FLAG PLACEMENT

SURVEYING THE SCENE 47

YOUR FIRST JOB

much. Hitting one is not a tragedy. Usually you just put another hole in it and you can put it back in place. Homeowners usually don't notice. The drain still drains, while a damaged sprinkler head just stops working. That they do notice.

Look around for anything else you need to avoid, like gas mains, electric lines, water lines, and flag those too.

Okay, you're ready to aerate. Start your engine. Ready, set, GO.

AERATING

I could talk in detail about how to run the machine, how to make it work, what the various mechanisms are, but there's little point.

The truth is that the only way you are going to get a feel for the machine is to go down to the turf dealer and try it out. Sales people are usually very knowledgeable and usually very good at breaking you in on their machines. Each aerator has its own features, characteristics, and operating controls. You need to become familiar with these as you shop. You also need to read manufacturer instructions carefully once you get it. By the time you do a few practice runs, you will know what a particular machine is all about.

All I can say is that it's not all that much harder than mowing a lawn, taking maybe a little muscle to move it around.

As far as the actual aeration goes, there's no particular corner of the yard to start on. Start wherever you feel like. I tend to do front yards first, then the back. It's your choice. There's no particular pattern to follow. Like mowing, you just need to make at least one pass on every part of the lawn.

Good machines have a zero turning radius. You can stop on a dime, turn the machine and move on. In that, you just pull back on the machine. The salesman will show you how to do it. It's like skiing in some ways. When you have to go onto concrete, you disengage the aeration and drive right over it. It would be a mistake to aerate the driveways.

The key thing to watch is the sprinkler flags. Go around them as you come to them. In the beginning, you'll probably give them a generous amount of space, then find yourself getting closer and closer as you become more familiar with the machine. Homeowners don't expect you to hit every inch of the grass.

You don't have to worry about putting too many holes in the lawn. In fact, heavily compacted areas and dry spots can use more than one run over it. A first pass will take out maybe 15% of the soil, and a second pass maybe another 3%. Then you start getting into holes inside holes. The only danger is if you are sitting and running the aerator in one spot for awhile. That can damage the lawn. I usually go over compacted soil at least twice because I like to feel good about the job I'm doing.

With the front yard done, you move onto the back yard. You may have to do some lifting and jiggling to get the aerator through the gate. Be careful not to damage the gate. It's not a big deal. I've never had anyone complain. Homeowners will tolerate a few dings on the gate. Just don't be obvious about it.

When you finish aerating, it's a good idea to turn the irrigation system back on and make sure you didn't break any sprinkler heads. (I do maybe 700 lawns a year and break maybe one or two heads. I'm careful about it, so it's not a big issue for me. If I do break a head, I tell the homeowner I'll come back one evening and fix it. And I do follow up.)

The main thing is to make sure you thoroughly aerate all parts of the lawn -- particularly the high-visibility areas.

Where you know there is going to be foot traffic -- near the walkway to the front door, along sidewalks, in the small area between the sidewalk and the street -- go over the area a couple times. These are the areas people will judge you by. When they get home, they'll tend to look over the areas they can see walking in, and may never get around

AERATING 49

YOUR FIRST JOB

to inspecting the rest of the grass. So do your best in the areas you know they will notice the most.

FERTILIZING, ETC.

With the aerating done, it's time to pull up the flags and apply the fertilizer with the spreader. Follow manufacturer instructions carefully and practice on your own lawn. If you got the B1 or B3 Pro spreader, put it on a setting of 3 for a normal pace or 4 if you are going to be moving fast over the lawn.

Here are couple of guidelines: One, it's always better to under-fertilize than over-fertilize. Too much can burn the lawn. Second, the rule is that you never pour the fertilizer into the spreader above the lawn. Do it on the concrete off to the side. Again, spilled fertilizer can burn that part of the lawn.

Then do the soil conditioning if the customer has agreed to that. It's the last thing you apply. On the West Coast, the conditioner is usually gypsum and iron. On the East Coast it's more often a pelletized lime treatment with iron added.

Soil conditioner you can use at full strength. You don't have to worry about burning the lawn when you pour it into the spreader. It's not a nitrogen-based product like fertilizer is. Just avoid dumping it in one area; that can hurt the lawn. If you have the B3 pro spreader, just put it on a setting of *8*, which is almost wide open. Spread it evenly and you'll be fine.

The last thing is to sweep the cement or get out your air blower and blow everything back onto the lawn. Make all walkways and driveways clean and neat. That's important to the customer.

You are done. Time to load everything back onto the truck, and do any last bit of clean-up you see.

GETTING YOUR MONEY

Many business advisors will tell you to be sure to collect your money from the homeowner as soon as you finish the job. If you feel most comfortable with that, then go ahead and do it.

I don't bother and I've never had any trouble with collections.

When I finish a job, I just make out the bill from the Client Card, and leave it in a letterhead envelope -- along with my cover letter, watering instructions, and turf tips. (Discussed in Promotion and Selling.)

If a customer is handy, I will give the envelope to him or her and ask for a check. Otherwise, I'll just leave the envelope in the screen, door crack, or anyplace that's immediately noticeable. Not stopping to collect speeds up my day and I've had very few people not pay me.

MOVIN' ON

With a little practice, all that should have taken about 20 minutes for a front lawn, or 45 minutes for a front and back. If the homes are reasonably close together, you should be able to average two front lawns or a front/back per hour. That's $70 to $90 an hour if you're making the maximum sale emphasized in the Selling chapter.

The entire focus in all this is to make the job go as quickly and efficiently as possible. Working well takes precedence over working fast, but the idea is not to waste time. A smooth loading-unloading routine, having everything in the right place, and not stopping to gab -- these all help. The more jobs you can do in a day, the more money you make. You should be able do 10 jobs a day -- but only if you are doing them as proficiently as possible. Make that a key.

So let's move on to that next customer...

YOUR FIRST JOB

CHAPTER 6

BIDDING THE JOB

We have talked about how much money you can make in this business. Now it's time to get down to just how you make that money on a job-by-job basis. Just how much can you charge the customer?

To answer that, we will look at pricing suburban lawns and huge estate lawns. In suburban lawns, we'll look at what to advertise for a front lawn aeration, how much to charge for both front and back lawn, and how much to charge for applying a bag of soil conditioner. This conditioner, as you will see, can be a big profit center for your business.

The focus here is getting the most money possible out of every job. The guidelines I will give you are based on my own experience in Southern California and on what I know to be national averages.

We will look at pricing on three different levels:

- **PLAN A** ... the low end of the pricing scale. It's what I call the *Market Share* plan and what I consider to be the minimum you should charge. It's a reasonable place to start in this business. The priority here is getting a strong share of the market in the first place and building a customer base. You won't get rich. But you will penetrate the market, make decent money, and position yourself for big dollars in the future because you will have established that strong customer base.

BIDDING THE JOB

- **PLAN B** ... the profitable level of the pricing scale. It's what I charge for most jobs now. I call it the *Profit Share* plan, and it will make you good money. It's a good price level to jump to when you are feeling comfortable with the quality of the job you are doing, when you are comfortable that new customers will keep coming in, and when you realize the advice you are giving your customers is getting pretty good as your turf knowledge increases.

- **PLAN C** ... the big profits level of the pricing scale; what I call the *HiProfit Share* plan. Whether you can charge this will depend on your market and the answer to the question: What are people willing to pay? It's appropriate when you know you are doing the best aeration job in town and when your value as a turf expert makes you worth the price. Unless you've found a bonanza, you have to be careful not to price too many people out of the market. But know that the price you are charging is still reasonable. You are doing quality work. You should be paid well for it.

The key in setting your price is that you want to hit both ends of the market. You want the customer who is very price conscious, and also the customer who will spend whatever it takes to make his lawn lush and green. The profit of this business is in volume and in appealing to everyone considering an aeration.

Having established those pricing levels, let's start taking a look at one of my most profitable markets.

SUBURBAN LAWNS

In the suburban market what you are after is that low end customer -- lots of them.

When you start out, you want to go to the lower end of the scale. The goal is getting your market share. You want all the customers you can get. You get them by charging a lower price. The objective here is to build as much of an initial customer base as possible.

This is the Plan A approach, reflected in the *Suburban Pricing* chart.

SUBURBAN PRICING			
	FRONT LAWN up to 2,000 sq.ft.	**FRONT & BACK** up to 3,000 sq.ft.	**ADD $5** per 500 sq.ft ↓
PLAN A *Market Share*	$32.50	$55	
PLAN B *Profit Share*	$37.50	$60	
PLAN C *HiProfit Share*	$40.00	$65	

The low-end figure for aerating a front lawn is $32.50. This is what you advertise on your promotional literature. Then you find out if the customer has a back yard and explain that your price for doing both lawns is $55. So you have already nearly doubled the size of the check you are getting from the homeowner and there is more coming -- when we talk about selling soil conditioner too.

Figure you can do a little over two lawns an hour (two fronts or a front/back). With that, you are already making $40 to $50 an hour after all expenses -- and this is the low end of the pricing scale.

Launching a business this way is very common. I was talking to the district manager of a major corporation the other day and we agreed. Let's say you and I start a business together. The first year we go out and get the business at any price. We know it's important to stay busy and get our market share. And the only reason we are charging that low price is that we want to stay in business.

Then when you feel more confident, you build up to a higher price, namely Plan B. You are now advertising $37.50 for a front lawn and $60 for both lawns. This comes as you begin to feel you are going to be in business a long time. You are starting to get more business than you need. You can be more selective about customers now.

At this point, you'll probably even see a little business turned away. But know this: In the long haul, successful businesses don't take all the

BIDDING THE JOB

business that comes their way. You have to turn down the unprofitable business because what's important is doing the business that meets your goals: namely, making money.

If you are beginning to feel successful -- if the market looks like it will go higher -- then you can start looking at the HiProfit Plan C pricing range of $40 and $65. Again, you want to be careful not to price too many people out of the market.

With these guidelines in mind, let's talk about a few other aspects of bidding these jobs:

- **Minimum Price.** Your front lawn aeration quote is your minimum price. I don't recommend doing any job for less than that. Many of your competitors may have a minimum charge and won't even come out and drop the machine for less than $50. Some big lawn companies have policies like that. This may give you an opportunity to under-bid that price and break into the marketplace. So one of your first projects needs to be a little research on what your competitors are charging so that you can meet or beat that price.

- **Lot Sizes.** The *Market Share* prices I've given you are aimed at suburban neighborhoods with lawns of less than 3,000 square feet. I usually know from surveying a neighborhood just how large the average front and back lawn is and key my advertised price to that. If the lawns in your area are larger than 3,000 sq.ft. then you need to get out your tape measure. For example, if you have a 50'x50' front lawn and an identical back lawn, you are up to 5,000 sq.ft. That's what the last column in the *Suburban Pricing* chart is for. To the bid, you add $5 for each 500 sq.ft. above 3,000 sq.ft. In this example, that's an additional 2,000 sq.ft. or another $20 on your bid price.

- **Decimal pricing.** I advocate using the decimal mark on flyers and other promotions aimed at suburban areas -- $24.50 instead of $25. It's a marketing key. It gives customers an idea that I've looked at their lawn and analyzed how much time it would take.

- **Small Lawns.** Understand that every area of this business is profitable, so you don't want to neglect any of it. The average front lawn is very quick and easy. Takes about 15 to 20 minutes. You can do three an hour if they are close together. The average lawn (front and back) runs 45 minutes to an hour, because there's more running back and forth with equipment, fertilizer, and supplies. I've even been in situations where the lawns are super-small, say 200 sq.ft., and I've dropped my price to $22.50 (front) and $35 (both). What makes that profitable is the lawns are close together and I can do them very quickly. So seize any opportunity that you see in your area. I've gotten repeat customers off those tiny jobs too.

Let's go back for a moment to that Plan A pricing -- $32.50 for a front lawn. I want you to know that's cheap for the customer. He will spend nearly that much to get the oil changed on his car. And we are talking here about a service where you actually come out to the house and provide a service on their property. So don't forget to sell that, and you might look around for some other comparisons.

When I first started my business I did an aeration for $25 and got business. I raised it to $30 and still got the same amount of business. I tried $35. Now I'm up to $40. In hindsight, I don't think there are many customers I did at $25 that wouldn't have been willing to do it at $35. So keep that in mind.

You also have to remember that if you price it too low, you might move yourself out of the market because customers won't think that it's a quality service. We Americans are funny that way. We always want the lowest price and never trust the lowest bid!

So my real caution here is: Don't charge too little. Look at what your competitor is charging and find a price range that is both profitable for you and profitable for the customer. Remember that he is getting a job done that will improve the appearance of his property.

ESTATE LAWNS

Estate lawns are the big ones and they can be great profit centers.

I've broken these jobs into three sizes to give you some ballpark figures to work with -- 7,500 square feet (a 75'x100' lawn), 15,000 square feet (100'x150' lawn) and 1 acre (43,560 square feet or roughly a

BIDDING THE JOB

200'x220' lawn). My pricing ABCs for these jobs are reflected in the *Estate Pricing* chart.

The national average for aeration is a penny a square foot. You can also consider that as a guideline in bidding.

Plan A, at $85 for 7,500 sq.ft., is a very reasonable price for the customer. Actually, it's low for you. If you do an acre at $400 at that price level, you may well feel it is not enough, but you won't go broke. It's reasonably close to a reasonable price.

Plan B, the Profit level, is closer to the national average. At $150 for 15,000 sq.ft., you are right at a penny a square foot, and an acre at $500 is a little over a penny.

It will take you maybe an hour to do 7,500 sq.ft., and maybe an hour and 15 minutes to do the 15,000 sq.ft. job. (You save some time because a lot of the set-up activities are the same -- taking supplies/machine off the truck, turning sprinkler valves on and off, marking sprinklers heads with flags and talking to the customer.) You will find that the bigger jobs tend to be more profitable.

So how do you know how many square feet a lawn is?

One way is to get one of those little tape rollers that will measure out an area. A 100'x80' lawn totals 8,000 sq.ft. So if you are in an area where you have to go out and give bids because there are large lawns, then you need a tape roller. After that it just takes a little practice and a little multiplication to get a good estimate on all those irregular-shaped lawns.

One nice thing about estate lawns is that you are going to get these renewals over and over. These people care about their lawns. They are usually seeking quality over price. So it's a good market to push. When you have large estates, it's a good idea to go down and meet the people, get an idea what they are willing to pay, and give them a price for aerating their lawn.

In Plan C, you are now charging $175 for 15,000 sq.ft. It's good money. When you can add in an extra $20, $25 on the estate job, it really makes a difference on the bottom line at end of the day. With five or six of these a day, you can make an extra $150 a day.

ESTATE LAWNS

ESTATE PRICING		7,500 sq.ft	15,000 sq.ft	1 ACRE
PLAN A	*Market Share*	$85	$135	$400
PLAN B	*Profit Share*	$95	$150	$500
PLAN C	*HiProfit Share*	$110	$175	$600

What's important in estate pricing is to strike a reasonable balance between getting the most for each job and setting a price level that will bring the customer back each year. You probably won't see the full benefits of that until we talk about the beauty of Repeat Customers in the Selling chapter. Keep in mind for now that it is critical to do a quality job at a quality price that cannot be beaten by a competitor.

SOIL CONDITIONER

Selling soil conditioner is one of the major profit centers of this business.

Remember how we got the price of the job up from the advertised $32.50 to $55 by including the back yard? Well, add in two bags of soil conditioner and you now have an $80 job that takes only a few minutes longer. Sell three bags and you're up to $92.50. That's a big jump in what you are getting from each customer. So consider it well.

We will talk more about how to sell soil conditioner in the Selling chapter. In the *Soil Conditioner* chart, you will notice that I've set the ABCs on that as $11.50, $12,50, and $13.50.

Let's see how that builds your profits.

BIDDING THE JOB

If you are buying this in bulk (discussed in Equipment and Turf chapters), it is costing you $3 per 50-pound bag. Bought by the bag from a local turf distributor, it can cost you $6 to $7. So the key here is getting a good price on the conditioner to begin with. You want to at least double your money on this. So even if you are spending $6 a bag and getting $12, you are meeting that goal.

Know that this is a good deal for the customer. A lot of times people will be paying $14, $15, $16 for a bag of quality fertilizer. If you are putting on fertilizer free and adding soil conditioner for $12.50 a bag, you are definitely providing a benefit that will appeal to your customers' wallets.

On estates, the lowest price you can offer someone is $10.50 a bag, but feel free to negotiate. You simply have to read your market. If you do a 15,000 sq.ft. lawn for $150, and you sell the customer 15 bags of soil conditioner at $10+, you've just increased the price of that job to $300. And a lot of times they will be willing to pay $12.50 a bag. Take it. In fact, that's what I always charge. With that small shift in the soil conditioner price you have just increased that $150 job to $330.

SOIL CONDITIONER

50-lb. bag gysum with 4% iron

covers 1,000-1500 sq.ft

SUBURBAN

PLAN A	$11.50 a bag
PLAN B	$12.50 a bag
PLAN C	$13.50 a bag

ESTATES

7 bags or more . . .

$10.50 a bag

That's the way you make money in this business. And the customer is getting a lot out of it. The immediate benefit of conditioner is a deeper greening of the lawn, and he has just paid you less per bag for fertilizing and conditioning the lawn than he would have to pay for high-quality fertilizer at the neighborhood nursery.

You can take a 50-pound bag of soil conditioner and because it has no lawn-burning nitrogen in it, you can apply it to an 800 sq.ft. lawn with no problem. You can stretch that same bag up to 1,500 sq.ft. and still get good results with it. So on 3,000 sq.ft., you can get by with two bags. If you can sell three bags, do it.

Thus, if you use the soil conditioner sales, you are going to make a lot of money. If you just sell the basic aeration plus fertilizer you'll be making money but walking away from the big profits.

AVOIDING THE TRAPS

This chapter and the Selling chapter are all about getting the most reasonable profit you can from each job.

In the whole delicate art of negotiating with the customer, it's time to warn about some traps you can fall into. I know because I've fallen into most of these at one time or another.

The first has to do with what I call Lawn Consultations. This comes at the point where you are becoming an expert on different grasses, can spot problems, and can offer the homeowner some good advice on caring for his lawn.

In the Promotion and Selling chapters, we will talk about some good reasons for giving this advice away free when you are talking to the customer on the job or on the phone at night.

But when a potential customer calls and asks you to come out and give him some free advice on his troubled lawn, it's a different story. He's not hiring you yet. He's just dangling this carrot in front of you so that if your advice happens to work, he might give you an aeration job later.

Don't bite on it. Know this: If they need help with their lawn and they call up a nursery, the nursery is going to charge them a service call charge. Do the same. Your time is valuable too. I recommend you charge at least $20 to $25 for that service call. Then use the techniques outlined in the Selling chapter to make sure you do get an aeration job out of it too.

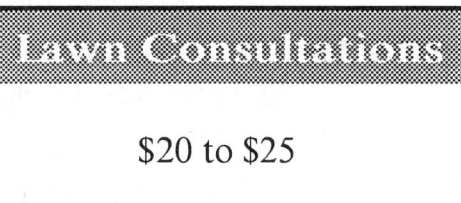

Lawn Consultations

$20 to $25

BIDDING THE JOB

A second trap comes when someone will call and say: *My neighbor and I want a deal to do the aeration together. How much will you cut the price to do both jobs?*

The trap here is that you may be tempted to go below what you've already decided is a reasonable price. It's not a serious trap. If you can pull the jobs together easily, then okay, go ahead and do them. Offer them maybe $5 off on each lawn. Just be sure to keep the price at a level where you are still making money.

And before you do give away the game, do some negotiating of your own.

What I do in these situations is to first explain that when I set the price they may have seen on my flyer I had already considered the fact I was going to be doing many jobs in that area. I note that my normal aeration price is $40 for the front lawn, so the price they saw was already a discounted price based on my being in the area.

About 85% of the time that will remove their objections. If it doesn't, then you can use the techniques outlined in the Selling chapter to build the value of the job and stress the quality of your work. What you're doing there is making the price worth it.

If the customer doesn't budge, you might consider giving them $5 off. You might even wait a day before you do call them back and lower the price. But don't lower it much, because that gets you into a third trap which is even worse.

This one comes when you are aerating a lawn and the guy from next door walks over and says: *Look, you've already got all your equipment unloaded here. How about doing my lawn for half price. It'll only take you a few minutes.*

It's tempting, because the guy is right. It's not going to take much to do the job. But let me tell you a story about the problem that comes up here.

I had a very good customer, a woman referred to me by a lawn care company. While I was aerating her lawn, this neighbor came up. He had a bermuda lawn, and bermudas tend to look very good after an aeration. He was very price conscious. He noted that I was already there and wanted me to do his lawn for $15. I tried to get him up to at least $20. He wouldn't budge. And frankly, I was already feeling a little indebted to the guy. The lady had a pet tortoise in her back yard that I didn't want to mess with and he had moved it out of the way for me.

So I did his lawn for $15. Only took me about 8 minutes or so. It was a real small lawn. I made him promise faithfully not to tell anyone about the price I had given him.

It came back to haunt me the following spring when I called the woman about a repeat aeration. She was real upset. She knew what I'd charged her neighbor. She didn't want to pay more than $30 for front and back. Why didn't I just do it when I was in the neighborhood like I did for him? I tried to explain it, but all she knew was that her neighbor got his lawn done for $15.

The bottom line is that I lost more business than I gained. I knew I could have done her lawn twice a year. Instead, I lost her business permanently.

So watch that trap. You are running a business and you can't give your service away. Since then, I have walked away from these jobs.

You have to remember these don't add up to much anyway. Ten cheap customers at $20 each amount to $200. You will feel much better at the end of the year when you've made your $20,000, $30,000, or $40,000 that you didn't do those people because they didn't help you meet your goals. And let's face facts. At $15 a lawn, you are not going to stay in business long.

A FINAL NOTE

The important issue in the area of bidding each job is not to give away your shirt. You want to charge people a fair amount of money for the services you are offering them on their property.

Many people are willing to pay for good service. You are out there working reasonably hard. Don't feel guilty about making good money for providing a service they need.

BIDDING THE JOB

64 A FINAL NOTE

CHAPTER 7

PROMOTION

Promotion is the process of bringing you and the customer together; getting his attention. It covers everything you do -- with flyers, advertising, etc. -- to let a potential customer know you are in business and convincing him to call you about aerating his lawn.

As always, this book will emphasize the least expensive ways of attracting customers. Thus, the focus is on using flyers, signs, and getting referrals. We will also talk about newspaper ads, cold calling, writing lawn articles, and county fairs.

Be aware that the old adage is true: It does cost money to make money. Promoting your business does cost dollars. But what we show you in this book is how to spend $200, $500, $1,000 and bring in $1,000, $2,000, $5,000 worth of business.

STANDING OUT!

Marketing. Promotion. Advertising. Those words can't be emphasized enough. To build a profitable business quickly, you must be constantly thinking of new ways to attract customers all the time. You have to think of yourself as a marketing powerhouse. I can guarantee your bank account will be grateful.

PROMOTION

Many gardeners and lawn care people don't even get into this. They just want to cut grass and run with the cash. They don't think of themselves as businessmen or marketers. If you take that extra step, if you look at yourself as a salesman offering the best lawn aeration service, you will bring in the jobs and profits that others let slide by.

At first, the going may seem slow. But constant promotion breeds accounts. Think about it. If 10 new accounts bring in $600, and 20 accounts bring $1,200, then just a few more will bring $2,000, then $3,000. If you market yourself aggressively, you can realistically achieve $1,500--$3,000 a week by using the ideas and tools in this chapter. It's work, sometimes 12-hour days, but the market is there. The trick is to get that market headed your way. That's what your promotional money is spent to do.

Good marketing is even more important in the lawn aeration business than most businesses. Many people aren't familiar with the benefits of aeration, or haven't even heard of it, or can't locate an aeration service. For some reason, the public doesn't easily wander through the Yellow Pages or look in the newspaper. Many people call me and say: "Boy, was I glad to get your flyer!" or "I've been thinking about getting my lawn aerated and didn't know who to call." In your advertising and promotional efforts, you want to make certain that people know what you're selling and that they call YOU to buy it.

Lawn aeration promotion is a two-part process. One is the information side. You often have to make the customer aware of what lawn aeration does and how he benefits from it. Secondly comes the sales side. You have to make the customer want you, and only you, to provide that service.

THE CORE MESSAGE

The key to any successful promotion program is to focus attention on a product or service with a simple straight-forward message, and then deliver it over and over again. I call this THE CORE MESSAGE.

In this business, the core message is: *Sir, I provide the best lawn aeration service available. I have the best equipment. I have the experience. I will not let you down. I am a lawn care expert. In short, I'm a professional, and I'm going to be around to answer any questions you have about your lawn long after the aeration job is done.*

Everything you do -- in person, on the phone, with your promotional literature -- is aimed at delivering that message. It is the core, the heart, of all your promotional efforts.

Now, let's begin to look at the various tools you have available to promote your aeration service and draw those eager clients in.

PROMOTIONAL LITERATURE

By far, the most effective and least expensive marketing I have done is with promotional flyers I've left on doorsteps.

In the beginning, all my business came from flyers. Even now, as other forms of long-range promotion have begun to pay off, 60% to 70% of my jobs (including repeat customers) originated from the door-to-door distribution of handouts. It should be the mainstay of your promotion efforts.

In this section, we will look at various types of flyer formats and sizes, provide you with some strong suggestions about what to put on a flyer, and discuss different ways to distribute these handouts for the best results.

Actually the word "flyer" is a misnomer for what we are going to be covering. We use it because it's a familiar term and it gets across the idea. What we mean is any kind of printed promotional material that can be handed out to encourage people to call you about an aeration job. It's inexpensive. It works.

THE BILL CARD

So let's cut to the chase.

The first thing I'll tell you about is what I have found to be the most effective flyer-type format for getting the customer to you.

I call it the PEDROTTI BILL CARD.

PROMOTION

I've coined that term for the handout because it doesn't quite fit any of the normal categories. It's not exactly a flyer. It's not exactly an advertisement. It has elements of both. What I can tell you is that the quality of the Bill Card definitely impresses customers. They do respond to it. They do call about jobs. And that, of course, is the goal of all marketing approaches.

Think for a minute about your normal sort of flyer. It's on an 8 1/2"x11" sheet of paper. Usually a bright color. Sitting on the doorstep with other bright flyers. It's flimsy; hardly worth lining the bird cage with.

Now let's look at the **PEDROTTI BILL CARD**:

- *Size.* First, the Bill Card is half the size of a normal 8 1/2"x11" sheet of paper. It's just right for someone to glance through quickly and get the message easily. It has the economic advantage of getting two promotional pieces printed on one piece of paper. Printers call this "Two Up."

- *Weight.* It's not printed on your normal lightweight paper stock. This is what makes it stand out. The standard flyer is printed on 20-pound paper (which means that 2500 sheets will weigh about 20 pounds). The Bill Card is printed instead on 110-pound paper stock, about the thickness of most paperback book covers. It's the quality of the paper and its strength that immediately sets this hand-out apart from the crowd. The heavier paper stock doesn't cost much more than the normal paper. In a subtle way, this card and it's quality delivers the message that your customer can expect a quality job and a quality service.

- *Paper Color.* It's white, strangely enough; or a light buff color. The simple truth is that a white background is easier to read and slightly cheaper. Years ago, white was the only color available. Then colored paper became the rage. Marketers used yellow, green, pink, blue, anything that was available, to capture the customer's attention. Now, white's unusual again. (Note: If you do get the irresistible urge to use colored paper, don't use a fluorescent-colored paper. Fluorescents do not convey a

THE PEDROTTI BILL CARD

WANT A SMART WATER SAVING IDEA?

Do What the Pros Do — Lawn Aeration!

Aeration is a process which relieves compaction of the soil and allows oxygen and water to enter the root zone. Tines penetrate the soil and eject cores onto the lawn surface. After aeration, your lawn will hold in moisture longer, so you can water less often. It will also decrease the level of water run off from 30%-50%.

Lawn aeration is very reasonable, so call today!

A-1 LAWN AERATION
571-2884

Your front lawn estimate below includes fertilizer.

Most front and backyards aerated and fertilized for only '60!

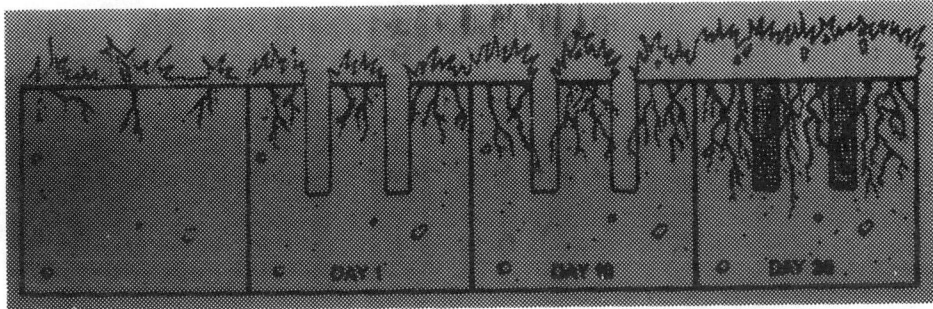

WHY AERATION?

- Watering savings of over 60%
- Provides root zone with needed oxygen
- Stimulates root growth and improves fertilizer absorbtion rate
- Increases turf's strength and disease tolerance

Ask us about our gypsum/sulfur treatment to revitalize your lawn from San Diego's saline water. This additional treatment raises the pH of the soil and allows a deeper green color without excessive growth.

PROMOTION

professional image and are harder to read than any other colored paper.)

- *Type Colors.* The most efficient use of funds is to print with one color. Green type is good, because we are, after all, talking about green lawns. Or you can go to two colors -- a little more expensive and a little more impressive. I suggest green ink for things you want to stand out, like a grabber headline, your logo, your phone number, your art work. Brown ink works well for the other promotion information on the flyer. My experience is that one-color Bill Cards have produced as much business as their prettier two-color cousins.

The Bill Card has worked well for me for a lot of reasons. It can bend into a door jamb. You can put it in a nook or a cranny and use some tension by flipping it over in half. It'll stick in the door crack or screen. It's easy for the customer to grab quickly.

In some residential areas, you find so many door hangers and flyers that the people get really irritated. Usually, the customer gets an 8 1/2"x11", 20-pound paper flyer that's not very heavy. If a wind comes up, it may not be sitting on the doorstep long, while the Bill Card, if it does happen to fly around, is substantial enough to live through it. I had one customer pick it up and say, "Hey, I found your paper on the street! Would you come aerate my place? How much do you want for my lawn?"

The way I look at it is that if the customer is going to get junk at the door, it might as well be quality junk.

This Bill Card has evolved over several trial-and-error years of trying nearly every type of flyer approach. It will create the bulk of your business. A few times during any given week, someone will call me and say: "I got your, uh, uh... you know." They don't know what to call it either, but they don't think of it as a flyer. I've had customers call me who say they never respond to flyers, but they are intrigued by this, uh, whatever-it-is.

FLYERS

Now let's talk about the more mainstream flyers. Obviously, I used them before I focused on the unique presentation of the Bill Card. They worked. I still use them occasionally -- mainly when I just want a few flyers to target a particular area with a particular problem.

For example: Recently I knew of a rural community where the water district was starting to get into drought problems. I had a friend whip up a quick water-saving flyer on his desktop computer program and made copies. Actually, when I started distributing, I thought I'd made a big mistake. The houses were farther apart. It was a pain. I only put out about 400 flyers. The response amazed me. I got about $700 of business out of it one Saturday and came back to do another $300 the following Sunday morning -- a good return on $35 worth of flyer preparation and copying.

So flyers do fly. And they come in a wide variety of shapes and sizes. The bulk of my profitable business has always come from promotional literature I've gotten into people's hands. Today, that's predominantly from the Bill Card, but along the way I've experimented with several other flyer forms.

Let's look at the choices you have:

- *Your basic 8 1/2x11, 20-pound printed flyer.* Covering about the same ground as the Bill Card, it tells the customer about the benefits of lawn aeration, offers a price, and gives him your phone number. The up side of these is that you can offer one-time special deals and work the name of a specific community in to break in there. The down side is that it can get lost in the clutter of other flyers. When I use them, I will insert the flyer into the Ryan sales brochure (discussed later) and use it for special promotions. The flyer/brochure combination both educates the homeowner on aeration and promotes my service as the only choice for getting the job done right.

- *Door Hangers.* They usually measure about 4" wide by 11" long with a hole and a slit at the top that allows them to be quickly hung on a door knob. The advantages: They can be put right

PROMOTION

where the homeowner has to reach to get in. They are hard to miss. The form itself is available at most printer shops. They are sold in bulk, with the holes already cut out. The disadvantages: They don't fit on every style door handle. They are very expensive. (Cutting the hole die costs almost as much as the printing itself.) In addition, people tell me they're tired of getting these on their door day after day. And because the card has to be narrow enough to fit between the door knob and door frame, the size of the text needs to be small. People really have to be interested to read it.

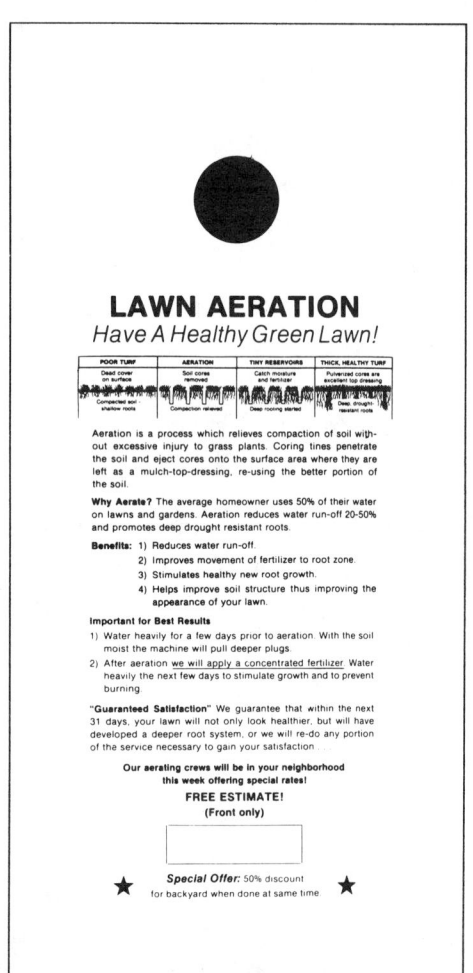

DOOR HANGER

- *Plastic Throwaway Bags.* You take your advertising piece or pieces, stuff it or them in a plastic bag, add a rock for weight, and seal it with a bag sealer. Then you drive by and toss these onto the driveway or doorway. The key advantage is that this can be done quickly. You can drive through a residential area and heave these out faster than any other kind of distribution. They are also waterproof. And you can use any format and weight -- a 20-pound paper flyer, a brochure, a Bill Card, or any combination of these. The disadvantage is that people dislike things thrown on their property. They arrive like litter and that's the way some homeowners treat them. If you believe the old saying that: "It's better to have a bad reputation than no reputation at all," you might try it. My personal view is that there are better ways to get the promotional job done.

- *Envelope Stuffers.* These contain the same information as the basic flyer, but cut down to about a third of a page; 3 1/2"x8 1/2". You use both sides. They will fit in a normal #10 envelope and give the customer the same sales pitch as the Bill Card or flyer.

72 FLYERS

What you do with these is to ask gardeners and other lawn care people if they will put them in their monthly statements. A Water-Savings approach can be effective in drought times. I've generated some new business with these, but I'm not convinced it's worth the time and money I spent on them. Still, they are worth being considered as part of a full promotional campaign.

WANT A GOLF COURSE GREEN LAWN?

YOUR GARDENER RECOMMENDS YOU DO WHAT THE PROS DO . . . LAWN AERATION!

Aeration is a process which relieves compaction of the soil and allows oxygen to enter the root zone. Tines penetrate the soil and eject cores onto the surface area where they are left as a mulch top-dressing. We will perform the work one to two days after your gardener mows. Then we can either use a regular fertilizer or a soil conditioner at a reasonable charge. The following week, your gardener will skip the lawn mowing so that the cores break-up and fertilizer goes undisturbed.

Most front and back yards aerated and fertilized for only $50!

• Please see reverse •

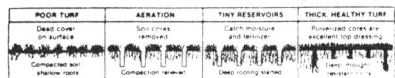

Ask us about our gypsum/sulfur treatment to replenish your lawn from the high salt content of San Diego's water. Our treatment raises the pH and fertilizer absorbtion rate of your soil. Our turf manager will be working for your gardener the next two weeks, offering special rates!

CALL FOR FREE ESTIMATE!

A-1 LAWN AERATION
SAN DIEGO, CA
571-2884

LAWN DETHATCHING ALSO AVAILABLE

ENVELOPE STUFFER

A key point is that communities vary. What works in one area may not work in another. In carrying through a full promotional effort, you may have to try them all to find out which works best in your area.

PROMOTION

The important thing is to NEVER slack off in your distribution efforts. This printed material, in whatever form, is likely to get you more customers than any form of promotion.

BROCHURES

Brochures are another major tool in your promotional arsenal, and they work differently than the flyer. Specifically, brochures sell your service or product, not yourself.

The primary use of these brochures is to educate the potential customer on what lawn aeration does. On each of them, you stamp your name, address, and phone number.

The best brochure I've seen is produced by Cushman-Ryan, a major manufacturer of turf equipment. It's entitled *Lawn Aeration*, and contains detailed information about the benefits of aerating a lawn. It is a fold-out color brochure, with excellent graphics and easy-to-understand text. There's space on the back to stamp in your name and phone number. The brochures now run about 5 cents apiece, and are bought in quantities of 500. I've provided the name and address for the company in Appendix H.

The brochures can be used separately or with your own Bill Card to generate business. It's more cost effective to use the brochure separately. These are especially good for putting on the counters of nurseries and other lawn care companies.

Or use them in an information packet that you send to the customer after completing his or her lawn. (We'll talk more about the information packet later.)

Brochures are also good to give to gardeners. Gardeners don't seem to hang onto a business card, but the brochures they can keep in the glove compartment of their truck. Ask the gardener to give a brochure to his customers who need aeration work done. Again, it will have your name and phone number on it.

These brochures are not usually cost effective in door-to-door distribution. Flyers and Bill Cards work better.

One exception is with large estate lawns, say 8,000 square feet or more. The advantage to using brochures here is that brochures aren't keyed toward quoting a price as the Bill Cards do. The estate customer tends to have more concerns than just price.

Estate owners will tend to ask more questions and want more details about the work to be done than the standard homeowner. Price is less of a consideration because these customers are looking for high-quality service and they expect to pay for it.

LAWN AERATION BROCHURE

The tough part sometimes is to get the brochures to these owners, particularly on estates surrounded by fences and gates. The best bet is to place the brochures on the entry gate or near the mail box. Remember: These are profitable $100, $200, $300 jobs, which can take as little as an hour or so to do.

These jobs do take longer. You may only get in five or six a day, compared with your normal 10 jobs. But once you are set up and aerating, you can give the customer a great deal and still make $150 an hour. And the large-lawn customers do tend to be more loyal. They are worth cultivating.

PROMOTION

FLYER CONTENT

By now, you should have a feel for the various promotional handouts and perhaps a budding decision on which one you want to use.

Your next logical question is: *Okay, so what do I write on this thing?*

My best answer is to lead you through the Bill Card I've developed over the years. We'll look at the points it makes in a step-by-step way and talk a little bit about working with printing companies as we go along.

It should sell *your* lawn aeration service. Many flyers are too information-oriented. They talk too much about the benefits of lawn aeration and not enough about the benefits of hiring a particular person or company to do it. Remember, this is your chance to sell YOU! Do it! Your card should be thorough yet simple. It should be readable.

In terms of content, the key to success in the lawn aeration business is to always use the word "golf course." The home aeration industry evolved out of the golf course industry. Those are the state-of-the-art lawns everyone can identify with. You want your potential customer to be thinking of golf course lawns when he's thinking about hiring you to aerate his lawn.

Starting at the top, it's important to have a good heading that gets people's attention. I've used: "Golf course green on your side of the fence" and "Want your lawn to be golf course green? Do what the pros do." Both of these have worked well for me. Try different headings from year to year to keep them from getting boring. You'll find there is a small percentage of people who read your flyer every year and notice the differences. That might seem trivial, but remember that these are good customers and are the people you're targeting anyway. A repeat customer is a $500 job if he does it annually over 10 years.

You don't want to offend potential customers with such headlines as: "Your lawn looks like the waste dump down the street!" You want to entice them, not insult them. Lead them toward the promise of a better lawn and a better life.

BILL CARD CONTENT

GOLFCOURSE GREEN
ON YOUR SIDE OF THE FENCE!

Through the process of Aeration, soil compaction is relieved and oxygen can then travel to the root zone. Aeration Tines penetrate the soil and eject cores onto the turf surface where they are utilized as a productive top-dressing.

WHY AERATION?

- Watering savings of over 60%
- Provides root zone with needed oxygen
- Stimulates root growth and improves fertilizer absorbtion rate
- Increases turf's strength and disease tolerance

Ask us about our gypsum/sulfur treatment to revitalize your lawn from San Diego's saline water. This additional treatment raises the pH of the soil and allows a deeper green color without excessive growth.

Your front lawn estimate below includes fertilizer.

Most front and backyards aerated and fertilized for only $55!

A-1 LAWN AERATION

268-0193 or 571-2884

| Poor Turf Compacted Soil | Aeration — Compaction Relieved | Deep Rooting Begins | Thick, Healthy Turf! |
| DAY 1 | DAY 10 | DAY 20 | |

The first paragraph tells what aeration does. It is informational, but also very short. Remember that the brochure is your main informational tool, but you need this explanation here in case a customer doesn't know what lawn aeration is.

The next section asks why aeration is done, then answers its own question. It explains that aeration produces water savings, better root growth, and allows fertilizer to absorb faster. These are *features*. You

PROMOTION

need to balance them with *benefits*. For example: A feature is that lawn aeration saves water. The benefit to the customer is that it saves money. A feature is a better root system. The benefit is lusher lawns and less cost on reseeding. The feature is greener lawns. The benefit is that the owner doesn't have to spend as much on fertilizer. Most of these fall into the customer-spends-less category. Customers like that.

The next section "Ask us about..." talks about soil conditioner and introduces other services the homeowner might want to buy while you're doing his lawn. The soil conditioning discussed here is one of the major add-ons of the business. (We'll talk more about this in Selling and Turf chapters.) Constantly develop new add-on profit centers for your basic business.

Now introduce the cost for the front lawn. Forget about the back lawn for now. Set your flyer up to write in the price by hand. Never typeset the price. That way the customer knows it's unique to their property.

Then put a line about a front-and-back aeration offer. There are several approaches you can use here that all work very well.

1) Give a price on both front and back yards in the flyer. That's what I normally do. It lets the homeowner know exactly what it's going to cost when he or she calls. I think it's the most honest approach.

2) Offer a "half-price special" for doing the back yard at the same time as the front, without quoting a price. I mention it because my competitors have used this approach, but I think it just confuses the customer. So I recommend quoting a price.

Next, add your logo. Pay a local artist to prepare a good logo for you. If you can't afford a logo which would include your name, address and phone number, print them in yourself.

Then comes the art that shows what aeration does. This artwork is more important than the printed copy. This illustration has sold more aeration jobs for me than the rest of the flyer put together because customers can instantly see what aeration does. (If you're interested in using my particular illustration in your flyers or brochures, refer to Appendix F for details on purchasing the art.) Whether you pay an

BILL CARD CONTENT

GOLFCOURSE GREEN
ON YOUR SIDE OF THE FENCE!

Through the process of Aeration, soil compaction is relieved and oxygen can then travel to the root zone. Aeration Tines penetrate the soil and eject cores onto the turf surface where they are utilized as a productive top-dressing.

WHY AERATION?

- Watering savings of over 60%
- Provides root zone with needed oxygen
- Stimulates root growth and improves fertilizer absorbtion rate
- Increases turf's strength and disease tolerance

Ask us about our gypsum/sulfur treatment to revitalize your lawn from San Diego's saline water. This additional treatment raises the pH of the soil and allows a deeper green color without excessive growth.

Your front lawn estimate below includes fertilizer.

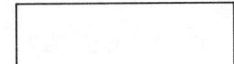

Most front and backyards aerated and fertilized for only $55!

268-0193 or 571-2884

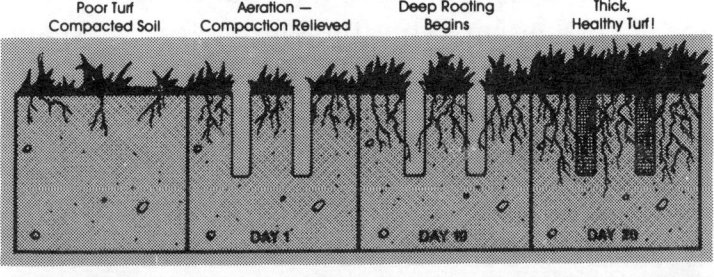

artist, or purchase the Pedrotti art package in the Appendix, you should have some art on the flyer. Eye-catching art does cost money, but over time it will pay off big.

One other thing you can do with your flyers is use the back to advertise other services. For example, if you want to get into slit seeding and dethatching (discussed in Turf), you might want to put some blurbs about these on the back. Make each a mini-ad, say about 3"x4" with a box around it, so that they don't detract from the lawn

PROMOTION

aeration you really want to sell on the front. Again, each of these should talk about what the service does and its benefits. Don't put a price on these. Let the customer ask. Too many handwritten or printed prices on the CARD dilute the impact of your major sell -- aeration.

What you use on the back does not have to relate to gardening. If you want to do window cleaning or carpet cleaning or trash removal too, advertise that. The point is that all you have to pay for on the back is the price of ink and that's not very expensive. If you put out 10,000 flyers, it might cost $70 more for printing both sides. The key is to keep the back subtle. Don't let it compete with the front for attention.

Through experience, I'll offer you my own THINGS TO AVOID list. Some stock advertising phrases are more trouble than they're worth and they can hurt your credibility. Such as:

- *A free estimate, or free fertilizer.* Avoid the word "free" in your promotions. The word is over-used and more often abused. NOTHING IS FREE. Everyone knows it. A free estimate? Come on! At the moment you put the flyer on the door it's for your benefit, not the customer's, and you both know it. Free fertilizer? Perhaps more legitimate, but it's not free. You had to pay for it. If they hire you, they'll pay for it. Again, you both know it. The minute someone starts offering things free, a reader starts doubting the truth of everything else on the handout too. With fertilizer, I just tend to say it is included.

- *Guaranteed satisfaction.* It's a cute phrase. Many business books will say you should use it. I disagree. You can go crazy going back and forth to a yard to make sure someone is satisfied. The minute you guarantee satisfaction, you're going to be getting a percentage of customers who are looking not to be satisfied. It's an axiom to live by; it's to your benefit that your customers are satisfied. But don't advertise it. Just do it.

- *Our crews will be in your area.* That's so impersonal and corporate and usually just a hoax by a small kitchen operation trying to sound big. Better to give the customer a name, usually yours, or a partner, or your title. Or: "Our residential turf manager will be in your area" works well.

Now it's up to you. Sit down with pencil and paper and start drafting out a version of your flyer. Think about what you want to use as a headline. Think about what else you might want to say, points you want to make, how you might want to illustrate it. Once you have what they call a rough "dummy" of how you want it to look and what it will say (it has to be readable), then it's time to start looking for a typesetter, then a printer.

Shop around. Ask about prices for 1000, 2000, and 5000 copies and ask how fast they can do the job. Get at least five bids. The price differential between printers can be as much as two and three times as much. Make absolutely certain you compare apples to apples. Each bid must be for exactly the same paper, ink color, etc. And look for chemistry with the people you select. If you don't feel comfortable when you place the order, more than likely you'll find something wrong with their work.

A good print shop can help you select art or find you an artist too. A good shop can give you suggestions on your flyer, based on their experience with other flyers they've done. If you are going to follow the **PEDROTTI BILL CARD** format, give the printer a copy. It's faster if you can show them what you want. Once the ball is rolling and they've set up the type for your original flyer, you can usually order more with just a phone call. Don't leave your original paste-ups with the printer. It's your property and you'll need it if you find a better price with another printer.

One way to save money on flyers during your early days is to go to a wholesale paper distributor, buy your own paper, and give it to the printers. It's cheaper. Most printers will mark up paper about 30% or 40%. Many printers don't mind if you give them the paper. So, let's say you buy 3,500 sheets of 110-pound card stock paper for a recent price of just under $100. Through the printer it would cost $130 to $140 for the same thing. You can't blame the printer. They have to stay in business. But then again, so do you.

DISTRIBUTION

You might recall my mentioning that door-to-door distribution of promotion literature provides the bulk of my business.

PROMOTION

But once you have flyers or Bill Cards or brochures in hand, that isn't actually where you start your distribution effort.

Garden Shops

The first thing you want to do, in that first week, is to get your material out to garden-related industry shops. These include shops that sell and repair saws or mowers, the nurseries, the big turf shops that sell gardeners their equipment/supplies, and the lawn care companies that spray insecticides and herbicides. (More about these in the section on Referrals.)

It's possible you haven't even bought your equipment or supplies yet. No matter. Get your flyers out quickly to the people in the industry. Let them know you're in business. Get to these people early. Get out and talk to at least 20 shops or so. You may not have time to do it later.

What do you say to these people? Remember the core message from the early part of this chapter. It's the message you want to deliver when you talk to anyone about your business. You stress you are a professional; that you do a good job, that you have an excellent machine. You emphasize that you are dedicated to providing the best service to all your customers. Ask if you can leave your flyers or brochures on their counter.

A few rules: Don't take up too much of their time (or yours). Don't take them away from their customers. You're calling on them as a salesman would, and you're often going to have to wait until they are free to talk. Building a relationship with these stores is usually a slow process, and this is just the beginning. If you do get your flyers or brochures on the counter, it is a major accomplishment. (And even if you don't, these people are now at least aware that you are in the lawn aeration business.)

Door-to-Door

The best way to distribute your flyers or Bill Cards is to go into a homogeneous area like new housing tracts or older tracts. It's easiest for you where the homes are part of a planned neighborhood, because the houses are usually close together and they tend to have the same size lawns.

In the beginning, get out and distribute flyers yourself. It's good legwork and you're going to need to get your body in good condition anyway.

Put out flyers as quickly as possible. Don't stop to talk to homeowners. Just get the flyers out. Six hours are about the maximum productive time for this. Take a break in the middle, but limit it to about 15-20 minutes.

It's best not to do the distribution at night. People tend to resent that.

Don't do it alone. Even if you're on a thin budget -- as Woodie Guthrie once put it: "So thin you could read a newspaper through it" -- you should hire another person to distribute with you and pay them well. A strong 14- or 15-year-old would love to get $5 an hour to work with you. Give him a bonus if he can outdeliver you. It takes two people less time. It's also less monotonous because you can stop to talk now and then. Otherwise it can feel desolate.

Flyer distribution is a numbers game. Get a box with 2,000 or 3,000 flyers out in your first week if you can. Don't get upset if you don't get many calls. It's all in the numbers, and the flyer has residual value. People save it. If you break even the first week, you'll make up for it with residual calls in the weeks to come.

If you're getting into the business full time, consider putting out about 7,000-10,000 flyers a month. That's a big commitment. If you're doing this part time, then maybe you're shooting at 3,000-5,000 flyers a month. If you think at the end of the day, oh, we got out 500 flyers and now we're going to wait for the next two weeks and see what happens, then you are going to go broke.

You'll find there are certain areas where you put out a ton of flyers and get one lousy job. There are also certain streets, called *hot spots*, where you will get 10 jobs and take 10 minutes to put the flyers out. On the norm, figure getting about one job for every couple of hundred flyers on the door.

One major benefit of door-to-door distribution is that you'll get calls from the same streets. You'll be able to do several jobs in the same

PROMOTION

area. You'll have the economy of scales working in your favor. You won't lose time and money driving between jobs.

Some further tips on door-to-door flyer distribution:

- *Placement.* Try to put the flyer at eye-level or at least reach-level in the crack of door jamb, or in the loop under many front door handles. Imagine the scene: Guy comes home with briefcase or lunchpail in one hand. He's got a paper under one arm. The kids pulling at him. If he has to bend over to get your flyer, he's going to hate you already. Make it easy for him just to grab the flyer and sort it out with the rest of his stuff.

- *Screen doors.* Try to place it underneath the handle. If you tuck it in the frame and it slides down between the frame and the screen, the homeowner is going to get upset trying to dig it out of the screen door.

- *Garage doors.* Avoid them whenever possible. Stick with front entryways. People tend to resent junk on garage doors, but in America's love/hate relationship with advertising they've almost become conditioned to expecting this junk at the front door. (And remember, this is junk to most people until they become excited about doing something for their lawn).

- *Mail boxes.* NEVER place advertising in them. The U.S. government has laws against using mail boxes for anything except mail. The law says you can't put anything on top of or attached to the mail box and specifies a $500 fine.

Now, suppose there are people outside and they start asking questions about lawn aeration as you distribute. What do you do?

It depends. If you're distributing flyers, then you go straight into the direct sales approaches we talk about in the next chapter. If you have someone else distributing flyers, then you instruct them to do this: Be polite, and be brief. Have them tell the customer what they know about lawn aeration and how it helps, and that if they have any other questions to call the resident turf manager. If there are people out front, put the flyer in their hands. That way you know they have it. If there's a gardener on the site, make sure he gets one too.

Other Possibilities

There are a couple of other places you can be putting your flyers and Bill Cards to attract customers. They include:

- *Car Windows.* You can do this at shopping centers, grocery stores, hardware centers, etc. Don't put them on windshields. People get irritated about that. Instead tuck them between the glass and the car frame on the passenger side, facing the driver. Go to golf courses and put flyers on the cars there, particularly if your flyer emphasizes "Golf course green" lawns. Everyone knows golf courses are top-of-the-line. There are lots of older people there who would love to have grass that looks like that.

- *Bulletin Boards.* Some supermarkets and lawn care centers have them. Keep your eyes open. Post your flyer there if you see one, particularly in your own neighborhood.

I haven't mentioned Direct Mailing of flyers for a reason. It's not cost effective. Don't do it unless you have the cash flow and a small team working for you. This is for a bigger business operation. It costs you much less to distribute your flyers than to have the Postal Service do it.

Okay, now that we have the flyers/Bill Cards out, let's look at the other promotional tools you have for bringing the customers in.

PROMOTION

TELEPHONE POLE SIGNS

Another surprisingly effective medium for promotion is posting signs for your business on telephone poles. It depends on the area, and you'll have to do some test marketing. This is not so effective in tight urban areas. People seem to get irritated and tear them down there. But in rural areas (where the homes are too spread out to make flyer distribution cost-effective), it can be an amazing bonanza.

Go to the hardware store and find a plastic "For Sale" sign. Take it to a silk-screener found through the Yellow Pages. Get bids for copying your artwork (see illustration) onto an 8 1/2"x12" piece of plastic like the "For Sale" sample you take along. Silk-screeners know where to find this plastic. Don't buy the plastic too thin, or you'll have a tough time stapling your signs up.

Another choice is to use heavy 110- to 140-pound paper for the signs. It's cheaper; 1,000 signs printed in green ink will only cost about $60 as opposed to $400-$500 for the plastic. Paper has the disadvantage of weathering faster, but your sign will usually only stay up a month anyway, so it's not a major problem.

Consider using white letters on a green background. Leave a 2" minimum white band at the bottom to write in your phone number with a wide-pointed black felt marker. Write in the number yourself rather than having it printed. It adds a personal touch.

You should be able to have a thousand of these signs made for about $400, or 40 cents apiece as a rule of thumb. Don't buy more than 1,000 signs to begin with. If you can find a silk-screener to give you a good price on 200 or 300 signs, then go out and put up a couple hundred.

Get a staple gun hammer that fires a staple when you hit it against the telephone pole. A good one is distributed by Swing (Model# HT50A). You can put up a sign in less than a minute.

Find wood telephone poles. They're the fastest and easiest to work with. You can staple a sign up in seconds. Stay away from city utility and light poles (which are usually metal and involve mucking around

TELEPHONE POLE SIGNS 87

PROMOTION

with a bunch of tape). Cities seem to be more sensitive about these posters, while telephone companies usually take a no-harm, no-foul attitude.

Just don't cover up any of the telephone company's signs.

Post your sign on main traffic arteries, and high-traffic corners where cars have to stop for a light or a stop sign. But also keep an eye out for high foot-traffic areas. Put these up about every four poles on the arteries. While they are not as exciting as the old Burma Shave signs, the first one or two will get the attention of a potential customer and he may be ready to write down the number by the fourth or fifth sign.

Put them up facing the on-coming traffic, so that the driver can see them off to his right. There will also be some areas, such as a narrow two-lane road, where they'll be just as effective on the opposite side of the street, to the driver's left.

Put the signs up about five feet off the ground at an angle facing where the driver will be about 30 to 50 feet down the road.

Sometimes the signs will stay up for as long as three or four months. There are other areas where people will take them down, but if they generate enough business they are worth replacing every couple of days.

REFERRALS

To build a solid business, you need to develop a base of people who will refer business to you. Flyers and signs are the quick avenue to customers; referrals are long-range.

Referrals come from three major areas: from gardeners, from other lawn care professionals, and from your own customers.

By way of definition, gardeners are those who are on-site, providing regular maintenance service. The lawn care professionals category covers a lot of ground; including nurseries, saw/lawnmower repair shops, tree-trimmers, and shops that sell irrigation supplies. It also includes those specialty companies such as Chem Lawn and Orkin Lawn Care which periodically apply insecticides, herbicides, and fungicides.

Look for the smaller lawn care companies that might be more willing to work with you.

It will take a while to build up these fellow businessmen's confidence in your work and convince them you are a professional. But the careful building of a referral base is well worth the effort. The more referrals you have, the less time and money you will have to spend on signs, flyers, and other promotions.

You'll generally find a higher grade of customer through a gardener or a lawn care company. These referral customers have already made a commitment to good care of their lawns and to hiring the best people they can find. These are people who are service oriented. They appreciate good work and are willing to pay for good work. They also know what bad work is.

When you come in as a recommended professional, you are already one step ahead of the game. Just be sure you don't abuse the trust of those who recommended you, because if you do, you'll find this very profitable business disappearing faster than a rabbit at a magician's convention.

Gardener Referrals

One way to find gardeners is to keep your eye open at convenience stores, fast-food restaurants, anywhere they might go to take a break and drink sodas. Their trucks are easy enough to spot. They have lawnmowers and garden stuff sticking out of them.

Just introduce yourself and tell them that you're in the aeration business. Get their card while you're at it, so you can send them some information in the mail. Don't take up too much of their time. Just a few minutes. If you think you're going to get a big account by talking to them for an hour, you're wasting your time.

What you say to the gardeners is what you always say. Remember the core message? You are a professional, etc. You can ask if they'd be willing to refer you. If you created the little envelope flyers we talked about, you can ask if they will put that in their monthly billing. You can ask if they will carry a stack of the lawn aeration brochures in their truck and pass them on to customers if the subject of aeration comes up. Develop friendly relationships. Consider giving these gardeners something.

PROMOTION

Offer to aerate the gardener's lawn as a good-will gesture in exchange for his passing your material around to his customers. They love it! For once in their lives they're not behind the machinery. They get to be the customer. Sincere gift-giving is a big part of the American marketing scene. If you own a hardware store, salesmen give you premiums and compliments. If you own a stereo store, you receive demos, posters, and various other gifts.

One great giveaway is a T-shirt with the name and logo of your company on it.

When you meet a gardener, ask for his business card, note his shirt size on the back and send him one. If he wears it, he's advertising your business.

You can also place a small ad in a gardener tabloid and say, "Send us your business card, tell us what size you are and we'll send you a T-shirt." Your ad investment will more than pay for itself. Once you have a gardener's business card on file, call and talk about your service, and ask if you might send him brochures for distribution.

Consider the economics of your T-shirt trade-off. If you send out 100 T-shirts at $5 apiece and that costs you $500, you can count on having much more than $500 in business the next month. And it will continue forever.

Silk screeners print the T-shirts. Shop around. There's a great variation in what they'll charge. As a rule of thumb, get BVT Haines, Steadmen. Those are good shirts. Fruit-of-the-Loom isn't bad. Don't look for the cheapest. Make them good T-shirts that people will wear. Order the shirts in quantities of 24 of each size. Stick with large and extra large; mostly large. Remember, you have to buy about 75 shirts to get a good price break.

Treat the gardeners and the other lawn care people well. You might remember them at Christmas too.

Another way to find them is to get a direct mailing list of people in the profession. Most cities will sell you a list of everyone who has a business license in a certain industry, like gardening, doctors, etc.

Garden Shop Referrals

Getting referrals from companies in the lawn care industry can be tough. It'll take persistence. It can also be a bonanza.

You have to look at this as a long-range project. But again, as I mentioned in the brochure distribution section, cultivating these people is the first thing I would do, the first day in business.

Find out which lawn companies are doing their own core aeration and which would be willing to give referrals. Send them T-shirts. Deliver your core message. Keep contacting them off and on.

A few good companies referring their business to you could amount to a full time source for all the business you need. But don't rely on one company. Chances are you won't get a lawn care company that will say yes on the first day they meet you. Be pleasantly persistent. Over the long run it will pay off.

If you have a spouse or older children, they can use the Yellow Pages to call every lawn care company in town and send out literature. It's a great way to get family members involved and let them feel that they are part of the business.

Offer to aerate the lawns of these lawn care professionals. (You may need the practice anyway.) Show them you can do the job. Take along brochures and, when you finish the job, ask if they would be kind enough to hand them out and refer you to their customers. Have any other literature with you so you can answer any questions they might have. Leave your business card and take theirs.

Here's an example of how it works in practice (mostly verrrrrry slowwwwly):

We'll call the company SprayScape. They provide a full lawn care service to their customers. When I first started, I called them, told them I was in business, sent them a little follow-up note, gave them my business cards. The result: They couldn't care less.

Okay. Then I called them periodically over the following months to give them leads on people who needed their services. Result: they still couldn't care less. The only time I heard from them was when they had

PROMOTION

a problem with a customer they couldn't solve and gave the customer my phone number to get him off their backs.

Finally, after about a year, I followed up by sending them $40 worth of T-shirts, along with more of my cards. This time it worked. Suddenly they started sending me customers. I'm now getting about $400 a month in business from these people.

Be aware that a concern these companies have is that you might give their business to your friends. Let's say SprayScape did give you a referral. And while you're working on that, the homeowner asks where to get his garden sprayed for insects. Suppose you have a friend who does spraying and needs the business. You must, for the sake of ethics, refer the customer back to SprayScape. This is professionalism. Give your friend business from your own leads.

Customer Referrals

Your best way to get customers to refer you, of course, is to do a good job on their lawns. That's a simple marketing fact. You do good work and you'll get referrals.

The problem is that nobody cares how good a job you did. They only want to see results. They want greener grass. And sometimes Mother Nature, whimsical wench that she is, will decide that a lawn is not going to grow no matter how much fertilizing, soil conditioning, and aerating I do. The way I fight that is to do as much as I can to help Mother Nature along.

As soon as I finish a job, I send each customer an information packet that includes a cover letter, watering instructions, and turf tips. I've included copies of these in Appendices A-E. You probably have to modify these for your own area.

I go this extra step because I look at this as a long range proposition, not just a here-today, gone-tomorrow, tough-luck-about-your-grass job. It's to my benefit to send the customer information on how to care for his lawn. If the grass is happy, he's happy. And a happy customer is a chatty customer. Friends and neighbors drool. They will want the same for their lawns.

Invite the customer to call and ask questions about his lawn. You are demonstrating your expertise, and showing the customer you care and want him to be satisfied. You're creating reasons for a customer to call you year-after-year to aerate his/her lawn.

ADVERTISEMENTS

It's probably crossed your mind by this time that you should be putting some advertising in the local newspapers to promote your service.

Forget it! Ads are not as productive as the methods already outlined. If you want to try newspaper ads, do so in May. By and large, putting your money into newspaper advertising will be very disappointing.

There are some exceptions. The ad in a local tabloid aimed at gardeners and other lawn care people is one of them.

Stay away from **BIG** Yellow Page ads. You should be listed in the Yellow Pages book that covers your immediate area. Even if you can afford a small ad, budget no more than $120 a month.

Be prepared for an onslaught of calls from ad sales people to call when your ad (and sometimes your flyers) first come out. They will be selling ad space. Resist the temptation. Stick to your flyer and sign campaign.

TELEMARKETING

This is when you pick up the phone and start calling people in a particular area to try to get jobs. It's also known as *Cold Calling* because you know nothing about the person you're calling. (Some of them may not have seen a lawn for years.) But the object is to convince them to hire you to aerate their lawns.

Telemarketers use reverse directories for this. (These books list people by address instead of alphabetically). The phone company or Chamber of Commerce should know where you can buy these books. With them, you know the people's names and addresses when you call and you call only in a specific area -- to get a concentration of nearby jobs.

PROMOTION

What would you say? Introduce yourself, ask if the customer is aware of lawn aeration and its benefits. Offer the customer a special first-time introductory price for having their lawn aerated. Deliver your core message.

Make your calls short and to the point. Don't chat. Get the job or get on with the next call. Be courteous, and expect some abuse and direct hang-ups.

The lawn care industry has utilized, especially on the East Coast, professional telemarketing firms asking potential customers if a professional can come out to their homes and sell them a particular service. The price these firms charge is usually too high to be worth it. But if family members are willing to do this for you, try it. Pay them as you would any other employee.

This is a tough route to go. Use it as a last resort. But use it if you have to.

WRITING ARTICLES

If you happen to be any good at writing, write articles about lawn care and submit them to local newspapers. It not only gets you attention, it gives you a special standing in the community.

Send copies of your articles to the lawn companies that are tough to crack. Call them and ask for subjects they might like to see covered in your column or article. Interview them for the answers to the lawn questions. Quote them by name and company.

Admittedly, this is not something everyone can do. But if you can, you're sitting on a gold mine. And it's not that hard. Just look at an article in any garden magazine or tabloid, call up a few lawn experts in the area to get their views on the subject, tailor what you write to the problems of your particular area, and Bingo! It's like winning the lottery. Most newspapers love to have a homegrown column about lawn/garden issues in their area, written by a local person. You have just become the expert. Jobs follow.

COUNTY FAIRS

Here is an opportunity. Consider sharing the cost of a booth with a Lawn Care Company that doesn't provide aeration. Pass out your flyers, brochures, or Bill Cards. Demonstrate the benefits of aeration. Often, millions of people attend these fairs over a two or three week span.

Consider having someone shoot a home video of you aerating a lawn, making sure to show the before-and-after results. Then let this video sell your service for you, even when you are away from the booth. Get a book on how to shoot videos for business promotion from the library and do as professional a job as you can.

If your video is thorough and gives most of the essential information, then the person at the booth will not have to know everything about the aeration business. Any detailed questions should be referred to you at your office.

OTHER IDEAS

Try a magnetic sign on your truck if you don't want to have your company logo and phone number painted on your doors. You can remove the magnetic sign if you use your vehicle for personal use.

Point out the benefits of aeration to your local water utility company. Water-savings is a big issue these days. Encourage them to write an article for the monthly hand-out that most utilities enclose with their bill. Encourage them to quote you by name on the benefits. Even if they don't quote you, an article on aeration sets the stage when your flyer arrives.

A last idea: Offer free aeration to churches and temples. But there's a catch here. You only want to do this for those who are willing to let you leave your flyers available to those who attend services. Be honest about it. Go talk to those involved in church maintenance or the pastor. Explain you are trying to start up a business, that you want to show people what aeration does, and that both you and the church can benefit. Admittedly, the size of some of those lawns can be daunting

PROMOTION

as a give-away. But remember that churches with large lawns usually have large congregations and they tend to be a loyal group, appreciating service to the church. Do church aerations on Saturday so people can see the immediate result on Sunday. Do temple aerations on Fridays. After several days of watering, the core will break down. You want it to look spiffy.

SUMMARY

To summarize: What I strongly recommend for marketing when you are first starting up your business is that you go very heavy into the **PEDROTTI BILL CARD**, signs, and a small Yellow Pages ad. Begin building your referral base. Skip newspaper ads.

The funds you are expected to invest for flyers, brochures, and the information packet are a must. Signs are too, if you think they'll work in your area. The garden tabloid ad, T-shirts, newspaper ads, can come at about the point where you are starting to make it and are serious about doubling and tripling your business. Most other ideas can be tried last. Consider them experiments. You never can tell which idea is going to take off.

The important thing is that you do have to market yourself. Loudly and proudly. No whispering. You have to shout!

CHAPTER 8

SELLING

In Promotion, we got the customer's attention with the PEDROTTI BILL CARD or a flyer or a sign. Now it's up to you, the salesman, to convince the customer to hire YOU to do his lawn.

That's what this chapter is all about. Selling. It will cover various sales techniques, teach you a sales approach for sizing up a potential customer's objections quickly, and show you how to lead the customer into hiring you as quickly as possible.

The focus here will be selling on the phone -- usually in response to a Bill Card or flyer. Approximately 90% of your business will come that way. Later sections will talk about selling door-to-door, handling referrals, and how to get the most sale from each customer.

Many people consider *sales* to be a dirty word. Some people have an aversion to the whole idea of selling. But in simplest terms, the better your sales skills are, the more money you will make in your business. And the goal here is to make you a lot of money.

IT'S AN ATTITUDE

Selling is more than just a collection of techniques and things to say to a customer. It's a frame of mind. You need to be thinking of sales

SELLING

all the time. You need to be thinking of new approaches on how to turn each conversation with a potential customer into another job. There will be rejections. People will say no. It's part of the game. But if you are thinking of sales -- how to do it; what's working -- then eventually, with persistence, you will find several approaches that work well for you. It's where the profits in this business come from.

Developing good sales skills is important in any business, be it lawn aeration, computers, or going door-to-door with a handful of Fuller Brushes. These skills are as essential as a weapon in a soldier's hand on the battlefield. Without a weapon, the soldier is as good as dead. Without developing sales skills, the businessman might as well admit defeat before he opens his doors.

There are two main breeds of salesmen. Many people believe they are good at selling because they are persistent. They work long hard hours. They "try, try again". And they do sell. A second breed works shorter hours. They don't want to put much effort in it. So they develop selling to a fine art. These are the guys who work smart. There's also a third breed, the ones who work both smart and persistently. They're the ones with the large estates you're going to want to aerate. This chapter is dedicated to teaching you how to work smart. The persistence is up to you.

COMMUNICATION

Communication with the customer is essential in any business, but especially this one. Crisp communication is a major sales tool.

You can take a gardener who doesn't do that great a job, but who talks well with his customers, and he will be making good money. In fact, if you talk to any successful gardener, he'll tell you his biggest job is talking to his customers. If he could simply go out and take care of lawns, trim the bushes, and kill the weeds, the job would be easier. But there's more to it than that.

People expect professionalism and good service, whether in gardening or aeration. They want to hear about their yard and any problems you see. Remember that. It is a key for getting current customers to refer new customers to you. And that's where the long-term money is in this business.

Some general communications guidelines: Be polite. Don't argue with customers, even if they are wrong. Don't degrade competitors' work. (Sell your own superior turf knowledge and golf course-quality equipment instead.) Be brief in your encounters. Don't take up customers' time (or your time) unnecessarily. Read books and articles on communications skills. Be aware of what you are saying to customers and work to improve those conversation skills.

PROMPTNESS

Too often promptness is ignored in this business. People don't return phone calls. They don't show up for the job on time. They say: *Oh, I don't feel like it. I'm too tired. I earned enough this week; I'll call next week.* Many people in the lawn care industry are incredibly sloppy about it. They leave the customer hanging for days.

I want to tell you right now that promptness and reliability in dealing with customers are essential to your success. Make a habit of answering all messages immediately and keeping all appointments on schedule. If emergencies occur, calling to reschedule is absolutely necessary. Do it before the appointed time, not hours afterward.

Returning calls promptly will give you an edge over your competitors. Even more, it will create a relationship of respect with the customer that may get a repeat job next year and a referral.

I'm reminded of a lady in Coronado who called me recently. I returned her call that very afternoon. Some problems came up in my scheduling. I rescheduled immediately. She told me she was comfortable dealing with me because I had done everything she expected to find in a good service.

About the same time, she was having a painter come to her house. He never showed. In fact, in the three or four days of our conversations back and forth, he never showed. Each day, he was to arrive the next day to paint her windowsills. And didn't.

SELLING

Frankly, I don't know if he ever did paint the sills, but I do know I have built a level of credibility with this woman. When the time comes that I am offering aeration services in her area, I know it will be an easier sale because she already appreciates that I have responded to her as a professional should.

If you show respect for the customer's time and lawn concerns, they will show respect for your time and your professional attitude. You'll be amazed at how far that will go in getting your customers to refer other customers to you.

TELEPHONE SALES

Your phone is your #1 link with the customer and most of your sales will be made on the phone.

I can't give you a specific model conversation and say, "If he says this, do this." But I will provide some tips for making your phone conversations as smooth as possible, and always directed toward making the sale. The key issue here is to be professional.

I can tell you to avoid prepared scripts. They rarely work. For example, a friend of mine got a job selling encyclopedias door-to-door one college summer. He went through a week of training. He got the script. He learned all the lines and counter-lines that were supposed to bowl the customer over at the front door. Then he went out on the street. His first potential customer told him: "If I were dictator, I'd ban your company forever." It went downhill from there. Nothing worked.

The problem, of course, is that the customers never read his script. They don't care what a salesman wants to tell them. They have their own problems. You will always have to start with the customers' worries and address *their* concerns. Think in terms of what it is going to take to make the customer satisfied and your own success will follow naturally.

Don't worry. As you take calls you will develop your own natural style. Be honest, be sincere. Most of all, be yourself. Convey confidence, cheerfulness. Speak clearly into the phone.

Remember that the first thing you want to do is nail down the aeration job itself. That's your focus. Then you can move into other products or service you might want to sell. We will talk about that in the section on Increasing the Sale. For now, let's focus on dealing with the customer in getting that first job.

Phone Tips

Here are some guidelines for handling customers on the phone:

- Be prepared to respond to questions about lawns. Study the Turf Management chapter thoroughly. Know your grasses. Learn everything you can about turf. Take classes at a college or junior college near you. Gather information from the Agricultural Extension office in your area. It is your expertise you are selling here.

- Be in control. Don't let the customer take charge of the conversation. Find out what his concerns are. Respond to them. Get the job. Move on to your next call.

- Be focused. Listen carefully to what the customer is worried about. Steer him back to lawn aeration if he starts to drift. Answer his question. Move on to the next question. Make the customer stay on track.

- Try to avoid listening to long garden stories. Some people love to talk about their gardening. Lead the conversation back to aeration and the benefits of aeration. But do it subtly, without the customer noticing it's happening.

- Do tell your own stories. Tell the potential customer about successes you've had with specific lawns. They love stories, particularly success stories. Make your stories short. Include a benefit (water savings, etc.). Make your customer feel that he's going to get that benefit too.

- Don't make the customer wrong. Be polite and professional. An approach that works well is: "Oh, yes, I can appreciate that. That can be true. What you should also be aware of is...." Then you

SELLING

go on giving him other information that may change his mind. In short: First you agree that he's right, then you tell him he's wrong without telling him he's wrong. It's tricky, but fun.

- Go for the close of the sale. Learn to sense when his questions have been answered. Then ask: "So what day would be convenient for me to come out and aerate your lawn? How about Tuesday?"

Overall, your goal on the phone is to convey that you know your business. That you are a professional. That they are going to pay for that professionalism. That when they called you, they made the right call. They don't need to call anyone else. Their search is over.

A Customer Example

Let's take a look at this in action:

Recently, a customer called to get his lawn aerated. He saw my flyer pricing aeration at $37.50 for the front lawn. He didn't have a front lawn. He wanted to know how much for his back lawn. Sometimes I charge more for back yards because they're larger or harder to get to. In this case, I quoted him another $37.50.

Customer: "Gee, I want a better price than that."

Myself: "I can appreciate that. My normal price is $40 for the front lawn. When I go into a neighborhood, I lower my price to $37.50 because I know I'm going to be doing several jobs in the neighborhood."

(So I am telling this customer he's already getting a discount.)

Customer: "You know, all you're doing is coming over to my house. How long are you going to be here, five minutes? To poke holes in my lawn? I don't want to pay more than $20 for that."

Myself: "Sir, I understand your concern. But I run a very professional organization. I use the best and most expensive golf-course machinery in the industry. It's expensive to use, but I don't believe in giving you less than the best job and the best results possible."

(Don't offend the customer. Don't challenge him. Continue to give him more reasons to hire you.)

Myself: "In addition to your aeration, part of my service is that you can continue to call me with questions you have about your lawn. I'll give you my phone number. You can call me anytime during the year in the evening. I'll help you out and tell you anything you need to know. I can refer gardeners if you need one. Now, is Tuesday morning convenient or would Wednesday afternoon be better?"

(By then, that was all he needed to know. He didn't question me further. I had convinced him I was a professional and he could count on me to get his lawn looking better. I continued our conversation and sold him soil conditioner. I took what he objected to as a $37.50 job and turned it into a $47.50 job. This is how you make money in this business.)

Closing The Sale

The purpose of all conversations with a customer is to end them -- with a job. That's what the *close* is. It's where you raise the question that will force the customer to decide, YES-NO, whether he's going to have you aerate his lawn.

You have already seen one example of that. *Would it be more convenient for me to come out Tuesday morning or Wednesday?* This is called the Alternative Close. It gives the customer two choices, both of which seem to coincidentally wind up with you doing the job. This takes the customer's mind off the question of whether he wants an aeration and lets him decide something simpler -- which day.

Here are some other varieties of closes:

- The Assumption Close: *Would Sunday be a good day?* This sets up the assumption that the customer is, of course, going to buy. All he has to do to confirm that is answer some innocuous question: *Did you want to add soil conditioner too?*

- The Ben Franklin Close: This is when you draw a line down a piece of paper and list all the pros and cons of an aeration. Then you add up all the pluses and minuses and somehow they always seem to wind up in your favor.

SELLING

- **The Puppy Dog Close:** *Are you not buying from me because I'm: too Black, too fat, too tall, too short, too young.* It raises the question of whether the customer is prejudiced about you for some reason he shouldn't be. It works best accompanied by a sad look or a sad voice.

The best closes for this business are the Assumptive and the Alternative closes. They're quick. I just mention the others because they may come in handy some day too.

BUILDING VALUE

What went on in that phone conversation earlier was a sales process known as building value. It simply means building the value of what you are selling -- in this case, lawn aeration -- to the point that the customer feels grateful to get all that for what he is paying.

Car salesmen do it a lot. Ever noticed that the salesman will stand there for hours and tell you (as long as you'll listen), every little feature the car has, and how the car is so unique. Why do they do it? Simple. They are building value. You can see what you're paying for: air conditioning; this terrific brake anti-lock system; this extra little doodad here and there. The more you hear about it, the more you can see yourself benefiting from all the little goodies the car has. The salesman has built the value of what you thought was just another car.

The same goes with lawn aeration. Mr. Smith calls. He's thinking of aerating. But he wonders if he wants to hire you. He questions the price. He's not sure aeration is going to help his lawn. You, in turn, are talking in more detail about the benefits of aeration -- about water savings, about how the holes provide a deeper and stronger root system, about how proper fertilization produces a greener grass. You are building the value of aeration. If you have more reasons for aerating than he has for not aerating, you will make the sale.

You are also building the value of yourself as *the* person to do the aerating.

If you have a Ryan LA28 or equivalent machine, tell him that you came across one of the revolutions in the industry -- your aeration equipment. Tell him this machine, about the size of a jet ski, puts a hole every 2 square inches. Before the LA28, a good aeration job was considered to be a hole every 4 square inches. Your machine produces twice the number of cores as other machines. It also cuts a hole up to 3 inches deep. That gives grass roots more room to grow, makes the grass healthier, etc.

You sell your experience as well, your lawn knowledge, your desire to get professional results. Admittedly, this is easier when you've been in the business awhile and have some knowledge and experience. Yet even at the beginning, you can talk about how you've been involved in gardening a long time. Tell them you've been working on lawns for years. (You don't have to mention it's your own lawns). You say you were so successful you decided to go into it as a business.

Emphasize after-job service. This is a great clincher. Tell the potential customer of the information lawn-care packet you provide after a job is complete. Tell them you are a consultant who is available by phone in the evenings at no expense.

This is building value -- both of aeration and of you as the person to do it. It is putting so much icing on the cake that your customer will have to have you as his aerator. (And then make sure you deliver the professionalism promised when you do the job.)

Let me add to that phone story I told. Remember how the customer protested the $37.50 aeration price. Okay. So I asked him what he thought it was worth. He said: "I don't know.... $15 ... $20." That became my starting point. From there, I started to build value -- benefits, machine, greener grass, etc. -- until the job was worth $37.50, and eventually $47.50, to him. That's how building value works. It could have been a $20 job if I'd have been willing to do it for that.

DEVELOPING THE NEED

The following diagram was developed by a Dr. Bittner at San Diego State University. Bittner has a PhD in communications. His thesis work was about selling.

SELLING

Until his theory evolved, nearly every sales equation involved the three elements below. Various sales experts showed the sales cycles in different ways. Not everyone described them this way, but the principle was same:

>SHOW THE NEED
>>DEVELOP THE NEED
>>>PRESENT THE SOLUTION.

Now Bittner added another element to this diagram that we will talk about in a minute, but for now let's focus on these three sales elements.

The existing need is always the first element in a sales equation. You have to show the prospect he has a need. In lawn aeration, the customer *needs* when he's looking at drying or dying grass and wondering whether aeration will save it.

For some customers, you'll have to develop that need further. You talk about the holes giving the grass roots room to grow, the holes helping to keep the water from draining off the lawn, the proper fertilizing to make the grass greener.

SALES DIAGRAM

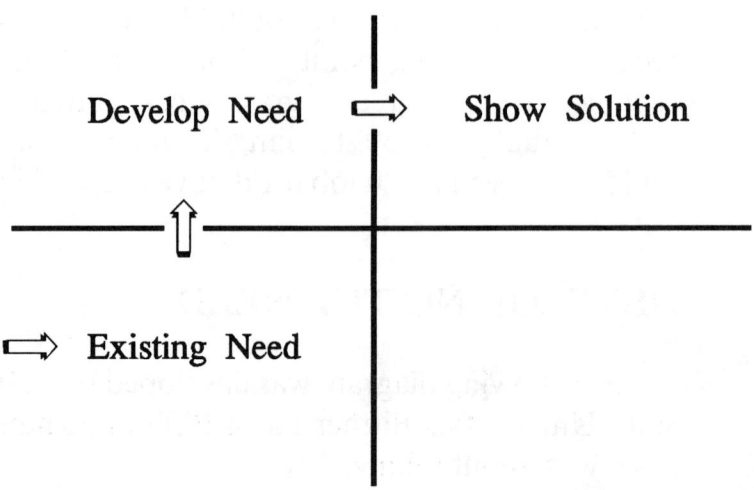

106   DEVELOPING THE NEED

All of it leads to the solution: Having you aerate and fertilize the lawn. It's the solution because aeration brings all the benefits talked about in the Aeration and Turf chapters.

DEVELOPING THE WANT

Dr. Bittner then takes this common equation a step farther to the word *want*. It's a very important word. Someone tells you they bought a computer? Now they could have bought a 20-megabyte computer. It would have met all their needs. But they spent even more money getting the best computer the store had to offer, the one with 100 megabytes. They may only use 20 megs, but they bought 100! Instead of spending $200, they spent $1,000. Instead of spending $300 on a simple printer that would handle all their needs, they spent $3,000 on a new, improved Laser Dazer Plus that would do everything except wash the dishes. Why? Because they *wanted* it.

As a salesman, when you learn to develop the want, when it really grabs people, you'll make more money.

One of the diagram's most important uses is to provide you with a framework to identify where the customer is at when he's talking to you. Is he at need? Do you have to develop the need? Is he ready for the solution? Is he already at want? Do you just have to close? Recognizing where the customer is can save you time in the sales process.

Bittner's approach isn't the only sales theory in town, of course. I'll also recommend a few books in Appendix I that should broaden your sales knowledge. But I can tell you that since Dr. Bittner taught this to me, it has worked extremely well in my lawn aeration sales. I now pass it along to you. Being able to sell your product well is the key to any successful business.

Here are some guidelines to tell how well you're doing. I consider myself a sales professional. Out of 100 calls, about 90 people will hire me. If your ratio is 75% or lower, your sales skills still need work. Remember, the bottom line is making money. The more *yes* responses you get, then the more jobs you have and the more profit you make.

SELLING

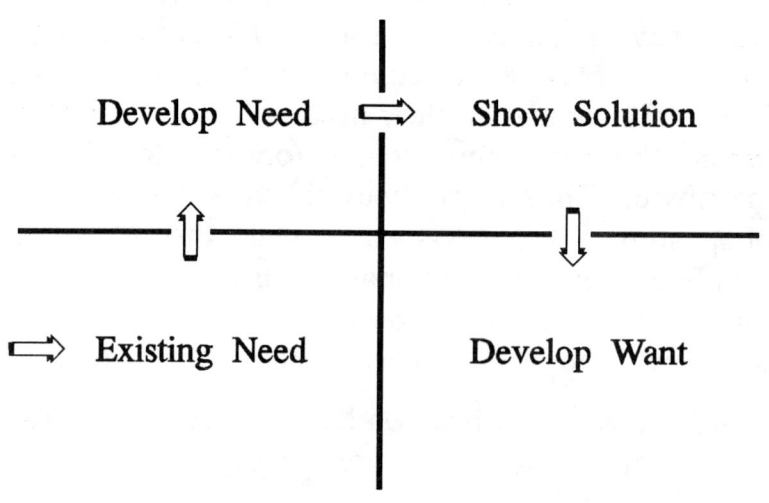

A final note: The better your skills, the quicker you can make the sale. Time adds up. Think about it a minute. If you can make a sale in five minutes instead of 10 minutes, you will have just saved five minutes. That, per 100 calls, is 500 minutes, or one eight-hour work day you did not spend getting the same amount of business.

But don't get too hung up on saving time. Don't rush the call. That puts people off. Simply do what you have to do to keep the sales conversation focused and bring the buyer to the close as quickly as possible. Efficiency will come with time and experience.

WHY PEOPLE BUY

Look at the bottom of the diagram, where we talk of Better and Worse. These are two main reasons why people buy things. Understanding these will improve your sales techniques.

One reason people are motivated to buy a product is that they feel it will make their life better. They will buy a microwave oven because it makes cooking easier. They will buy a fancy new car because they feel successful if they own a Mercedes Benz. They will buy a big computer instead of a small one because they think that too will improve their lives. It is the most pleasurable way to spend money.

But sometimes a stronger motivation for buying something is to keep things from getting worse. No one wants to go backwards. The last thing most of us want is for something to get worse. What do you think the insurance industry plays on? Do you buy homeowner's insurance to make life better? No, you buy homeowner's insurance to deal with the fear that things might get worse. People never want anything to get worse.

Remember *for better or for worse*. It's a theme in sales too. Sell aeration on whichever side of the equation works. If a customer's lawn looks terrible, the need is already there. You can make it better. If their lawn looks great, then you sell the idea of it staying that way. It's insurance. It provides a deeper and healthier root system. You will keep it from getting worse.

SALES FROM FLYERS

This is the major promotional medium suggested in this manual. The assumption is that a potential customer has seen a Bill Card or a flyer, and he/she calls you with questions. Now look at this in terms of the sales diagram.

Realize that the marketing is so strong on the PEDROTTI BILL CARD that you are already halfway to the sale. People responding to the Bill Card have already realized they have a need. They know the

SELLING

soil is hard. The Card shows how the service benefits the lawn. It offers the solution. So when people call you, many times they are very close to deciding that: yes, they do have a need. They believe your service, according to your graphics and your ad copy, will be their solution. They call you to verify that. So by going heavy with the flyers, you can *close* much more quickly because the potential customer has already gone through at least half the steps it takes for a sale.

The key here is to *listen*. Be buyer-focused, not seller-focused. Let the customer tell you what he doesn't like about his lawn. Tell him why aeration will solve that problem. Determine where he is in the sales cycle diagram and take him through the rest of the steps needed to make a decision.

For example, let's go back to selling a car. You're not going to sell a car to someone who hasn't test driven it. If you haven't built value, if you haven't given the customer the information he needs, then the customer will find some objection when you try to close. He'll say he doesn't know what he should do; that he has doubts about the car ... or about lawn aeration.

When that happens, you go back to the need immediately. Define their need further. Cover unanswered questions. Some people will say: "Yes, I know I want this. Yes, I want that too." And bang, it's over, it's sold. Others will say: "Well, I don't know if aeration is going to help my lawn." So you talk to them about the quality of your aeration, that golf courses do this quarterly, and that your equipment provides the same professional aeration that golf courses get. You go back to developing the need, stressing the importance of aeration and how it solves the problem. Then you go for the gut, for the pocket book. You close the aeration sale; you try to sell them on soil conditioner.

INCREASING THE SALE

What you want is the biggest money job, the most profit, out of every customer. Polished sales skills are what give you that.

When a customer *wants* the lawn aeration process, when you've shown the process is beneficial to them, you can then take the sales process a step farther and sell them the "add-ons." You've experienced this often enough. Sure, the base price of the car is $8,000 as advertised, but if you want air conditioning or mag wheels (or an engine), that'll be a little more.

In lawn aeration, there are several ways to expand the job through selling. The Bill Card emphasizes a price for front lawn aeration. Well, what about the back yard? It needs aerating too. If so, you have just doubled the job with this customer. Again, nailing down the full aeration job is the first thing you do.

In Turf Management you will learn about other lawn services such as dethatching, slit seeding, and renovation. If you want to expand your service to include these tasks, then you can talk to customers about these.

Fertilizer can be an add-on, but I recommend against it. It's too small a ticket. It only costs you about 25 cents a lawn when bought in bulk. Your competitor may not be offering it "free." You are. You are already a step ahead.

That sets you up for the good money add-on: soil conditioner. We talked about that in Supplies. What I use on the West Coast is a natural rock gypsum, with sulfur and iron in it. In the East, you'll be working with a pelletized lime product.

You should be able to tell right away whether you should back off. Aeration and fertilizer will improve a lawn. If the customer is interested in soil conditioner, then you have to tell him exactly what's in the soil conditioner and how it benefits the lawn.

My soil conditioner is a three-step sell. First, you explain that the gypsum will loosen soil. Second, you explain that sulfur helps lower the pH so fertilizers are more effective. Third, you add the clincher that the iron gives the lawn its deepest green. You tell the customer this package will last 3-5 months.

Some additional tidbits useful in soil conditioner sales:

- California tends to have a lot of salt in the soil, mostly from the water. This gives soil a high pH, which tends to block a plant's

SELLING

    intake of fertilizer. Gypsum leaches out the salt. The benefit is that this makes it easier for a lawn to absorb fertilizer. In a very salty lawn, the fertilizer often doesn't get to the plant at all.

- After the aeration breaks up the soil in a mechanical way, the gypsum continues to break up clay soil in a chemical way. This makes it easier for grass to thrive in the hard soils.

- The iron that's been added to the soil conditioner is what gives a lawn it's deepest green. In selling aeration, you focused on saving water and on healthier grass. You held back on the dark green and you use that now to sell the soil conditioner. Fertilizer will make the grass greener, but it is this iron addition here that makes it a deep green. This is usually what clinches the sale on the soil conditioner.

- In the East, the lime product works just the opposite way. There the problem is too little salt. The lime raises the Ph of the soil and makes it easier for the lawns to absorb plant growth additives. (Manufacturers and lawn care companies in your area should be able to tell you more about just what it does for soils in your area and how long a treatment lasts.)

Soil conditioner comes at the *want* level of the sales cycle. And it adds $10 to $15 to each job. That's a big percentage added to the profit.

DOOR-TO-DOOR SALES

To here, we've talked about selling on the phone -- usually from Bill Cards and flyers. Now let's look at actual door-to-door selling, either by you or someone you hire.

This is a method that works but takes more effort to organize and manage. It is not recommended. But if other parts of your marketing program aren't working or business just isn't coming in strong enough at the beginning, it may be something you'll have to try. Communities vary. In some areas, this may turn out to be most efficient sales approach of all. You can never tell.

In terms of the sales diagram, this is the toughest approach. Since the customer doesn't have anything in his hand, you have to start from the beginning. You have to create the need, develop it, offer the solution, and, if you're really good, get to the WANT level all in one shot.

So if you have a Saturday with nothing to do, and business hasn't picked up, then go door-to-door. It's ambition. If your heart's in it and you really want to do it, you can make yourself $200, $300, $500, doing the aeration as soon as you make the sale. It's hard work. But it can be done.

Again, hire someone to go with you. It helps keep you pumped up. In going door-to-door, you're facing a lot of rejection. Two people help keep each other motivated.

One approach you can use door-to-door is what we call the WIIFM statement; pronounced Wiff-em, meaning What's In It For Me?

In that, you identify yourself, give them a purpose for your call, talk about a benefit they could get, then respond to questions.

For example: *Hello, Mister Customer. I'm Robin Pedrotti of A-1 Lawn Aeration. I've recently been able to help Mr. Jones down the street with his problem of water running off the lawn and dry spots. I thought I might be able to help you. May I have a few minutes of your time?*

From there, you push the need: *Notice the dry spots. This will help you get water in the ground. It'll develop the root system. It'll alleviate those dry spots....* Etc. Talk about what's on the Bill Card, and in the brochure. This is what aeration is. These are the benefits. Point to the lawn and note the problems.

If you have a son or daughter or a cousin, someone you're close to in the family, this is a good opportunity for them to work with you. Take advantage of it. They can go door-to-door with you or by themselves.

When hiring someone outside the family, look for a natural salesman, someone who's already had experience selling Fuller Brushes or vacuums or whatever. You don't want to take someone who has no

SELLING

ability to sell and try to whip them into being a salesman. It's not worth it. Interview prospects to get the right person for the job.

Give your salesperson a basic knowledge of your business. Look at the grasses in your area, talk about each one. Explain how aeration helps each grass. Cover the equipment; how it does the job. Tell him to stress professionalism and good service. It only takes about an hour of instruction and training to get the important points across. An intelligent and natural salesperson will learn quickly and be able to close the aeration sale quickly.

One thing to watch out for when hiring people is what they will promise versus what you can actually deliver. The customer asks: "Is my lawn going to look better?" People want the cure-all. And the salesman says: "Sure, it will be beautiful." The truth is aeration may help the lawn, but does not in every case make the lawn perfectly green. Maybe the lawn needs more than aeration. It may need seeding. It may need all kinds of things it isn't getting. If your salesman is desperate for sales, he says: "Yes, your lawn will look great. I guarantee it." Then in three weeks, you may have an upset customer if the lawn needs more than aeration. Warn your sales people against such overstatements for the sake of your business and reputation.

Pay your help $5 an hour guaranteed, but tell them you'll give them a 25% to 30% commission on all their sales instead if that comes out higher. That gives them something even if there are no sales -- and much more if there are.

One last point that roughly relates to door-to-door sales: Say you are aerating a lawn and someone, a neighbor, comes up to talk to you. This is not an interruption. This is a potential sale. People do get curious about what you're doing. About 90% of the time, I can close these people in just a few moments and have another job to do.

SALES FROM REFERRALS

In terms of the diagram, referrals from gardeners and other lawn care professionals are the easiest to sell. These customers already want your services. Somebody they trusted has recommended you. It's like looking for an attorney. If you need a lawyer, and you ask around, and one attorney's name keeps coming up, then you are going to want that attorney. And because you want him, he is going to be able to charge you more. If the attorney called you, it would be a totally different situation.

Since these people already want you, your key question is simply: *What day is good for me to come out and aerate your lawn?*

Now, it might be possible these people aren't sure about aeration. You might have to go through the whole cycle of developing the need, building value, developing the want, and closing. It happens occasionally. Just be prepared for it.

If you get a referral from a chemical lawn care company, don't try to sell soil conditioner or fertilizer. Assume the company is already providing these services. Just quote them the price of a straight aeration job.

Always remember that the people referring you are putting their reputations on the line. Concentrate on good service. Build and gain trust in both the referring party and the customer.

SELLING REPEAT CUSTOMERS

I saved this for last because it is a sales area which doesn't come up until the second year. As business strategies go, I advise you to spend the first year using every promotion/sales technique we've already talked about to get every new customer you can.

At the start of the second year, you begin making that customer base work for you. You begin developing repeat customers, the profit-rich customers that don't cost you any more than a phone call to get.

My experience in California is that 35% to 40% will do business with me again in the spring. I always begin the year with these customers. Working part time these days, it takes me March, April, May, and June to get through these regular customers. That's nearly four months I don't have to spend any money on advertising at all. It isn't until late

SELLING

June or July that I start pumping the dollars back into getting more new customers.

Do you begin to see now why I recommend so much money into an all-out promotional effort that first year and how it reduces your costs more and more in the following years?

So how do you approach these customers?

Pick an area of city you plan doing next. Pull up the names of all the customers you had in that area the year before. Begin calling them. If you make 20 calls a night, you will be doing a huge marketing effort, because you are talking to people who are already buyers in that market.

What I say is: *Hi, Mister Customer. This is Robin Pedrotti of A-1 Lawn Aeration. I aerated your lawn last March, remember me? How are you? The reason for my quick call is that I wanted to touch base with you on your lawn. It's time to aerate again and I'm calling because I thought you would be interested in having that done. I will be in your neighborhood this Saturday and can drop by and do your lawn. Would that be convenient for you?*

If they say yes, then you try to add soil conditioner, and, as necessary, run through the whole selling game all over again.

There are couple of expressions I think are key ones. *"Quick call"* tells them you're not going to be taking much of their time. *"To touch base"* is a smooth transition into the sale and opens the door for them to raise any questions they might have.

The main thing here is to make this a soft sell. And a quick one. A 35% repeat base is a high number, but it still means two out of three people are NOT going to be interested in having their lawns aerated again. Don't waste your time with them. Your goal here is to sift through your customer base to find those who are going to be the cherries.

If they ask you to call back next month, then file the name for calling back then. If they say they only want to aerate every other year, then file the name to call back next year. But, if at any time you get the feeling they're just jerking you around, forget them. They are not the customers you're looking for.

A ploy you can use with people who talk of doing it later is to ask: *Do you mind if I give you my phone number in case you need me before then?* If you can get them to write your number in their little black book, they'll find you much faster than looking in the Yellow Pages. It's also good for those you're dropping. *Okay, I'm going to take you off my calling list, but if you do have a need for aeration, do you mind if I give you my phone number?*

Again, this is not a hard sale. It's not worth it.

Just how you keep track of all these customers is a subject discussed in the Seasonal Planning section of the Administration chapter. So don't worry about it now. It's not hard.

Hand-in-hand with this is the selling of biannual aeration -- the twice-a-year jobs. It's really the same phone call. The only difference is that the approach is now: *Hi, remember me? I did your lawn six month ago, and it's time to aerate again.* Then you begin selling the benefits of a fall aeration, the deep root growth effect then as opposed to the greening benefits of spring.

About half of my repeat customers go for a second aeration. This keeps me busy from September to November. That's three more months I don't have to spend money on promotion.

Again, this is something you don't begin concentrating on until the second year. And again, we will talk about how you keep track of all these people when we talk about client cards in Administration.

This repeat customer area is where the quality of the job you do and the quality of expert information you can provide them on turf really comes into play. That's why it's so important. Once you get customers to rely on you for lawn information, they won't want anyone else to do their lawn aeration.

For good work there's an even bigger bonus: As these people become loyal, they become your sales force. They start referring other people to you. After a couple years, that's 400 or 500 people out there who are a reference base for your business.

SELLING

One idea is to give them a novelty gift that second year -- a coffee mug or a tile to put mugs on that has your company name and phone number on it. Tell them it's for the office, where other people might wind up asking: *Just what is this aeration thing here?*

Repeat customers are golden. Treat them well, and do them first thing in the season. This keeps your competitors from eating away at the customer base you've worked hard to nourish.

THE BOTTOM LINE

If nothing else, I want you to remember that you are in business to make money. That's the purpose of professional sales skills. If you know how to sell, you will make more money. If you know some of the psychology behind sales, you'll be able to save time. And you'll be able to build profit because you'll know when you will be able to charge people more money or sell add-on products.

So don't be afraid to charge people money. Many times in the service industries, people underprice their skills. You will find that people who want a better, nicer-looking lawn will be willing to pay for it. They will also be more apt to refer you to other people because your service gave them what they needed and wanted.

For example: If you pay $10 for a dinner somewhere and you get an okay meal, and you pay $13 somewhere else and it's great, where are you going to go to dinner next time? Price is often not the issue. Quality is.

So develop an excellent service, and don't be afraid to charge for it. It's not unethical or ungodly to charge and make a profit. There is nothing wrong with getting paid well for providing a great service. What is important is that you provide *a quality service*. Most people expect to have to pay for quality.

SUMMARY

Good sales skills are often the difference between a marginally successful business and a profitable, booming business.

If you know some of the psychology behind sales, you will save time and be able to build your profits. You'll know when to charge people more money, and how to get the largest possible job.

Professional sales techniques involve: SHOWING A NEED, DEVELOPING A NEED, OFFERING A SOLUTION, and then: DEVELOPING A WANT. That's where the real profit is -- in *want*. This is what we have been talking about in a nutshell.

Keep the sales cycle diagram in mind at all times. Learn to distinguish where your customer is at in that cycle and what he needs to bring him or her to a close. Once you become adept at spotting where the customer is, you will stop wasting time, get the job, and be able to get on to the next customer quickly.

Remember that people buy to make things better or keep things from getting worse. Sell on both sides of that equation.

Lastly, remember you are in business to make money, and people expect to pay for good service. Give it to them and your profits will escalate.

SELLING

120 SUMMARY

CHAPTER 9

ADMINISTRATION

Ah, the paperwork. Sorry about that. But there's a business to be run here and how well you run it will make a big difference in how profitable you will be.

The sad truth is that many small businesses fail because the owners are so busy doing the job they just can't keep track of things. *We did deposit that check from Joe Smith last week, didn't we? Who was that guy in Hillcrest who got us three other customers because he was so impressed? I know I spent more than that on fertilizer last June; why does the IRS need a receipt? Well, I can't worry about that this morning, I have three more jobs to do.* In the end, they don't know what happened. They seemed to have a lot of customers. Money seemed to be coming in. But....

This chapter offers guidelines on how to avoid that. We'll talk about that in three parts. First, the office equipment and supplies you need. Second, operations: How to keep track of your customers and schedule your jobs efficiently. Third, record keeping: How to keep track of all the paper you need to get all the tax breaks you deserve.

Know this: The more efficiently you run the business side, the more time you'll have to make money aerating. The better you can monitor, track, and evaluate your business results, then the better you can make the business decisions that will improve those results.

ADMINISTRATION

OFFICE EQUIPMENT

We'll skim the obvious. You need a desk, chair, phone line -- someplace where you can work quietly, without interruption, and where you can keep all the records and paper that have to do with your aeration business.

Office equipment on your buy list:

Telephone Answering Machine

This is your #1 business tool and your most important. This is the answering machine that collects all the calls coming in from your prospective customers. It's the first thing you need to have.

Buy one of good quality. Expect to pay about $130 to $170. The brand I like is Panasonic (Model # KX-T1424). It's worked well for me. You don't need unlimited message time. One minute is about right. You don't want their life story; just their name, phone number, and request.

A sample message I leave on the tape for incoming calls is: *You have reached the answering service of A-1 Lawn Aeration. I'm sorry I'm not in personally to take your call. Currently I am out in the field performing aeration work. You can count on me to get the job done right. Please leave your name and your phone number at the beep and I'll be glad to call you back this evening. My office hours are from 7 to 9 at night. Thanks for calling A-1 Lawn Aeration, and have a great day!*

It's also important to change the message when you go on vacation to avoid losing jobs. One I use is: *You have reached the office of Robin Pedrotti and the A-1 Lawn Aeration company. I am on vacation and will be back on such-and-such a day. Please leave your name and your evening phone number at the beep, and I will call you back as soon as I return. Please remember that since I use a golf-course quality machine, I am one of the few people in the county who can provide you with the quality service your lawn deserves. Remember that quality is worth waiting for, and have a great day!*

Phone Lines

One phone line is mandatory. If you're going at this full-time, it will be worth having two phones and two numbers on the flyer so your potential customers don't run into a busy signal. Getting phone lines installed and extensions set up is one of your first priorities.

You may want to split the lines between business and personal use, between incoming (to the tape) and outgoing calls, or have both hooked up to answering machines. Either way you need extensions to your aeration office desk. Your phone is your lifeline to your customers.

Call waiting is not a good alternative to two phones if you are counting on your tape to give you your incoming customers.

The problem is that if a second person calls in while someone else is leaving a message, there will be a beep on the tape. If that beep overrides the phone number, you may have difficulty finding that first customer. Meanwhile, the second customer just gets a busy signal and has to call back anyway.

Call waiting could work if you know you are always going to have someone there answering the phone, such as a spouse.

Cordless Phone

A cordless phone isn't an item you need immediately. But when your business picks up and you find yourself spending an hour or more on the phone each night selling aeration, a cordless phone can increase your production.

I do a lot of talking with customers; selling aeration jobs, scheduling appointments. With a cordless phone, I can also walk around, make my bed, fold my clothes, fix dinner. It makes my time more efficient.

Expect to pay about $200 for a good model. I bought the top of the line, a Sony 10-channel cordless phone (Model # SPP-110). It's been

ADMINISTRATION

well worth it. It has two-button speed dialing for frequently called numbers, and I haven't had any trouble with the range. Check manufacturer's instructions for the best place in the house to install it to avoid interference.

Typewriter

It helps to have a good typewriter to prepare the cover letters, watering instructions, and Turf Tips that you give to customers. (There are samples in Appendixes A-E.) These materials are a major part of promotion and the image your company projects.

There are alternatives. Most of us know someone who types. Copy shops often have typewriters or computers you can rent time on. A computer, of course, serves the same purpose.

OFFICE SUPPLIES

Your most important up-front office supplies will be your letterhead stationery, envelopes, and business cards. They need to be impressive and professional.

Let's face it. When you're in the field, you're usually somewhat dirty, and wet. This is not a three-piece-suit world. Thus, it is going to be your promotional literature and your stationery that project the professional image you want your customers to have about the business you run.

A Logo

The heart of this is choosing a good LOGO or graphic symbol to represent your company. It should be striking and easy to remember.

Mine, of course, is A-1. You can pronounce it in two syllables.

You'll use your logo on all letterheads, envelopes, business cards, brochures, flyers ... on every piece of communication you use with the public. This adds value to your company. The recognition factor is extremely important in competing with other firms.

Your logo IS your company. Make it look good, but don't tie up a lot of money in it. If you or your friends are not artistic and you cannot afford to hire a professional graphic artist for the going rate, consider contacting a local college arts department. Ask the teacher to recommend his/her best graphic arts student for a job you'd like designed. You may get a much more enthusiastic response than from a professional and for a lot less money.

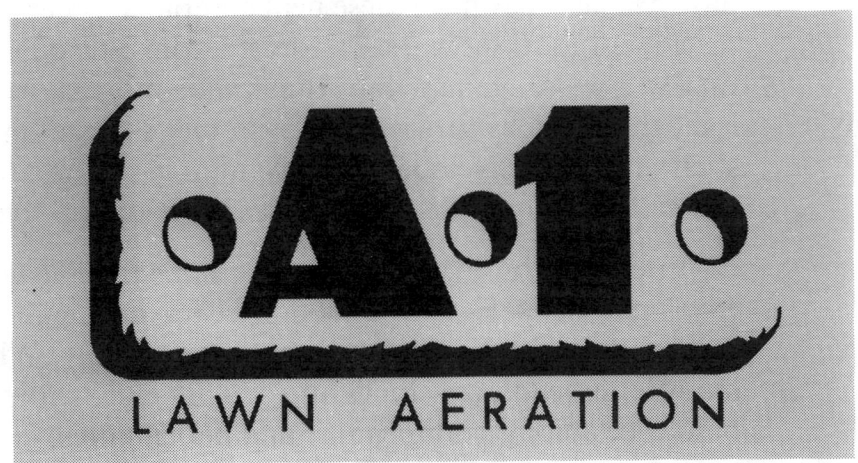

Another choice is just pick letters and numbers. A typesetter will probably charge $40 to set it up, and maybe another $40 to design a business card using it.

However, the easiest and fastest way to deal with this problem is to consider using A-1 Lawn Aeration as a company name and take advantage of the all the work I've done to develop the art for this logo. (See Appendix G.)

Stationery, etc.

For letterhead stationery, I suggest a light buff color, such as beige. Do it on 20-pound bond or 50-pound offset paper (Both specifications are the same.) Buy it at the wholesale paper store and give it to the printer.

Do your logo/letterheads in green ink. It works well with buff paper and green is unusual enough that the customer will recognize instantly

ADMINISTRATION

that it's from you. Do the letters themselves in normal black typewriter characters.

When you order envelopes, get the 24-pound solid #10 envelopes. Use the same color ink for logo and return addresses on them as you have on the letterhead. Most businesses favor window envelopes these days because they have these neat computer-generated statements that machine-fold to show the customer address through the window. But they will work against you. It can take more time to get the fold just right than it does to write the customer's name on the envelope. So stick with solid envelopes. You want to leave the envelopes at the door anyway. I rarely mail invoices unless I run out of envelopes in the truck.

Order your business cards at the same time as your letterhead and envelopes so you can get a good price on the complete package. Make certain you have this work typeset professionally. When you know how many letterheads, envelopes and business cards you want, shop for the best price among both printers and paper stores.

Billing Invoices

You need a couple of pads of invoices for writing out customer bills.

One I favor is the Rediform book (5L350). It has 50 invoices per book. There is a white copy of the bill for the customer and green/pink duplicate copies.

Rubber Stamps

You should buy a few customized and generic rubber stamps that will make your life easier and do a little public relations along the way. These include:

- MAKE YOUR CHECKS PAYABLE TO ... and include the name you want the check made out to, your address, your phone number. These are stamped on invoices left for the customer. I have all checks made out in my name.

- PAYMENT DUE IN FIVE DAYS. Stamped on the same invoices and preferably done in red ink.

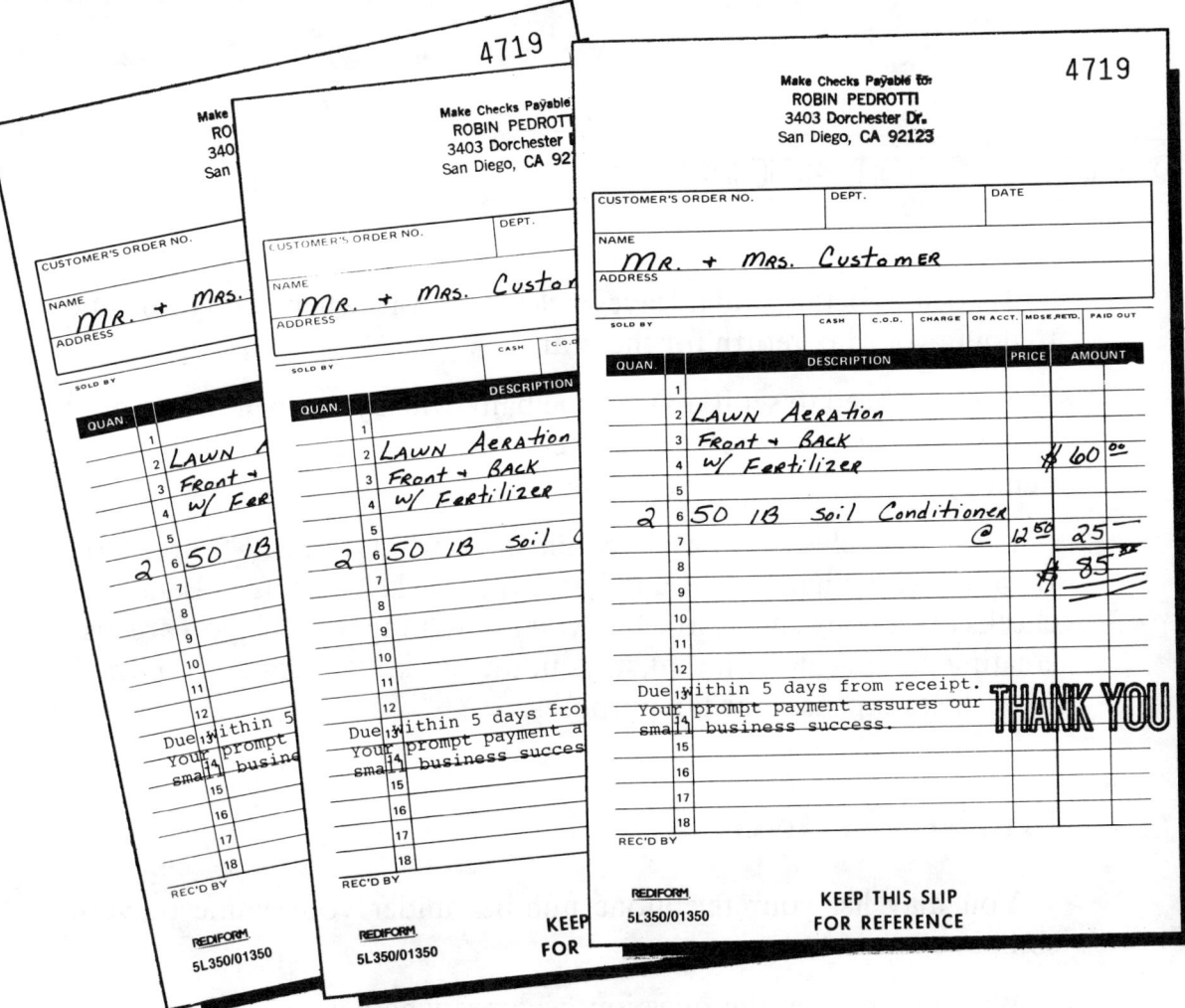

- THANK YOU ... Stamped on invoices when people pay you as you finish the job. It's a nice PR touch.

Other Supplies

A few other items on your office supplies Buy List:

- A package of 10"x13" Manila envelopes for storing receipts, invoices and other tax-pertinent records.

- A pack of 4"x6" cards for client cards.

- A metal box for storing those cards.

- An office stapler.

- A schedule organizer.

Bank Account

As a peripheral item in the setting-up area, you should open a separate business banking account. It helps you to track your income

OFFICE SUPPLIES 127

ADMINISTRATION

and expenses better, and it leaves a clearer record when you get around to doing your tax return for the year.

You will need to set it up with the bank when you open the account so that you can deposit checks made out either to you or to the business name.

In ordering checks, what I recommend is what they call "Three Up." It comes with a hard cover and has three checks to a page. Below the checks are a copy sheet, so when you are writing a check you are also creating a duplicate of it that stays in the book. It helps to keep track of business expenses for tax purposes.

PHONE LISTING

You may list your telephone number under your name or your company name.

With one phone, the question becomes whether to list it with the phone company as a business or personal line. As a business, you're usually able to get a small Yellow Pages listing -- which you do want -- but you won't have a personal listing under your name in the white pages without paying extra for it. The key is whether or not you want the Yellow Pages listing. If not, make it a personal line. It's cheaper.

It's easier with two phones. You list one as a business under your company name and the other as a personal line. You'll only get the business number in the Yellow Pages, but you can use both numbers on your flyers. Then use the business line for incoming calls and the personal line for all outgoing calls to customers. You pay a lot less for those same calls on your personal bill.

The Yellow Page listing is important. Small Yellow Page ads DO pay for themselves. Again, don't spend any more on Yellow Pages ads than it takes to get your name and phone in there.

The question becomes what category to list your business under so that potential customers can find it amidst the hundreds of other numbers listed under something like "Lawn Care."

The category answer depends a lot on what company name you choose. If you pick a name like A-1, then you'll be at the top of the more voluminous Lawn Care category anyway and you'd just as soon have your competitors lost in the shuffle. With another name that doesn't start with A, you could be the one getting lost and it may be worth trying to encourage the phone company to create a separate Lawn Aeration category for the listing.

I list mine under Lawn Maintenance. I could have done Gardening or tried to sound impressive in Landscape. The problem with those, however, is that you spend too much time weeding people who aren't looking for an aerator. So try not to confuse the customer.

I also once tried a listing under Rental Yards, on the theory I could convince the customer it would cheaper and easier for me to do job than for him to rent an aerator. I can't say it worked out all that well, but it's just another idea to offer you.

Okay, let's move on to operations.

CLIENT CARDS

Your 4"x6" Client cards are your links to your customers -- past, present, and future.

On them, for starters, go the customer's name, address and phone numbers -- a work number, an evening phone number, a pager number -- whatever you can get. Then note the job to be done: Aeration only? Fertilizer? Soil conditioner? Add the price agreed on.

You use these in planning out each day's work. Sort them into the order in which you are going to do the jobs. Carry them with you in the truck for reference. Use them in preparing your bill.

Make notes on the cards of anything you want to remember next time: A wife's name. A dog's name. The size of front and back yards, if unusual. Any special things to watch out for; like drains, gates, gas mains, irrigation peculiarities. You might even decide the customer is a jerk and you don't want to do his lawn next time.

Change the color of the cards each year -- say, orange one year, green the next. Use yellow for customers attracted by your Yellow Page ad.

ADMINISTRATION

```
Mr. Customer                           999-0202
6969 Anywhere St.
Yourtown      USA


                      Front + Back    60—
AM                    2 50 Soil Con.
8-12                       @ 12 50   25—
                                     ___
  Dog's name Duffy                   85—
  [Check under door mat]
```

That way you can tell instantly the year you are working in, or the year you took on a particular account, and how.

We'll talk about what to do with these cards at the end of the day when we get down to Record Keeping.

SCHEDULING

Time management. Efficient scheduling. These are big words for simply saying that the more jobs you can do in a day, the more money you'll make. And the number of jobs you can do depends on how well you schedule out your day's work.

In the morning, or the night before, go through the Client Cards for the day's work. Plan to do all jobs in the same area one after the other.

Glance at the map. See which one is easiest to get to first, then second, then third. Then go to another area.

On a regular basis you should be able to schedule 10 jobs a day. I've done as many as 15, but it depends on how far apart the jobs are, how many are fronts only, and how many are estate lawns of 10,000 square feet and more.

If you see that one job is out in Timbuktoo, you may want to do that last or reschedule for a day you are in that area. (But don't dodge too long. You make money here too and customers don't like waiting.)

Make avoiding traffic a key issue. If you know you'll hit traffic in one place at 3 p.m., then flipflop things around to do that job earlier or later. The whole idea is to get as many jobs done as possible and stay out of traffic jams.

And don't promise specific arrival times to your customers. All the utility companies promise is morning or afternoon. Do the same, and stick with it. Or call to make sure a change is okay. It helps keep your customers happy and their goodwill is one of the long range assets of your company.

SCHEDULE DIVIDER

SCHEDULING 131

ADMINISTRATION

I use a schedule divider, a vertical file, to organize a week's routine. (See illustration on the previous page.) As I get the jobs, I drop the cards in the day slot that the job is going to be done. Then all I have to do is grab the cards for the day and begin organizing my route.

With your Client Cards and schedule divider, you can speed up your operations a lot.

RECORD KEEPING

Good record keeping must be done from the very first day you are in business. There are two purposes. One is making sure you are getting your money from customers and the second is making sure you have all the records you need when tax time comes.

Tracking Unpaids

Let's start with the first, and go back to the Client Cards and the Rediform book.

The white copy of the bill is already in the customer's hands.

If the customer paid me on the job, I tear out the yellow and trash it. The pink stays as a permanent record in the invoice book. I write the check number on the pink, and the receipt number on the check.

At the end of the day, I sort out the Client Cards and put the Paids into a separate box for "Done" accounts.

If the customer hasn't paid, I take the Client Cards and keep them in a separate file. When the check comes in, I tear the yellow out of the invoice book and put the Client Card into the DONE box.

That's it. You are done with these Clients Cards for this year.

But remember, these cards are critical for keeping track of customers. You need to save them in a box specially designed for storing for 4x6 cards. At this point, you just put them in the box unsorted. They tend to fall in there chronologically. But you will need them later. So make sure you save them.

There's a couple of record keeping things to do at the end of each day.

One is to put any receipts for supplies you've bought during the day into a big envelope. These receipts are critical. At tax time, you can only deduct expenses that you have a record of.

The second is that if you are making any check deposits into your bank account, you want to make a photocopy of all the checks first. I tend to shrink them to 65% so I can get three or four on a page. Do two copies of each page. This is one of the simplest ways I have found to keep track of my income for the IRS.

Tax Records

As far as keeping records for the IRS is concerned, I have some good news for you. You've already done it.

You can get as complicated with your tax record keeping as you like. You can buy a three-ring binder with insert folders or an accordion file, or you can store receipts in folders, filed by the month. You can set up a ledger sheet and track all income and expenses. You can set up a cash or accrual accounting system.

But all you really need at tax time is:

- A record of how much money you earned;
- A record of expenses you had in running your business.

If you give your tax accountant a statement of income and drop the envelope of expense receipts on his desk, he will be able to do the rest.

You have already tracked your income in two ways: (1) the pink invoice copies in your sales book give you a record of all cash and check sales; and (2) the photocopies of deposited checks give a record of customers who paid by check.

Similarly, you have also kept track of expenses by: (1) saving the receipts on everything you bought for the business; and (2) with the duplicate copy of all checks written (the back-up copy comes as part of the checkbook).

Now it just gets down to the other deductions you can take now that you are a full-fledged business.

ADMINISTRATION

Tax Deductions

This is an area you have to talk to your tax accountant about. As a starting point, recognize that you have two different kinds of write-offs -- operating expenses and depreciable items.

Operating expenses are the day-by-day costs you incur. These include fertilizer, soil conditioner, stationery, envelopes, other office supplies, truck repairs, mileage you drove working the business, photocopies, and any interest on business loans. In short, anything you spent money on for the business.

Depreciable items are big ticket expenses the IRS requires that you write off over several years instead of deducting the full price in the year you bought them. Your aerator is the major example there. If you spend $4,000 on it, the IRS will probably look at it as equipment that will last five years and will only let you deduct $800 in each of the five years.

In your first year, you'll have significant Start-Up costs. Keep track of all expenses and let your accountant decide whether each one is an operating or a depreciable expense. You make out better if it is an operating cost because you can deduct it right now.

The other thing to look at is writing off a percentage of your rent or mortgage as a *home office expense*. The way it works is: Let's say you use one room strictly for your aeration office. Then let's say that room is one-sixth of the entire house. If you pay an $1,800 mortgage, you can deduct $300 of that (1/6) as the cost of maintaining an office. You can also look at whether you are using half or all of the garage to store equipment and supplies. Just be aware that the IRS is paranoid about this, so follow your own accountant's suggestion on this.

Remember that you don't have to make a profit to take deductions. You can operate at a loss for three years before the IRS may begin to believe your business is not much more than a hobby.

A Tax Warning

You are going to make a lot of money in this business, and your first tax bill could be a disaster. Here's why.

You are most likely to be running your business as a self-employed individual. When you do that, the government mandates that you make quarterly tax payments based on your estimated income. However in your first year you won't have to do that. You won't have to file until tax time on the next April 15.

For example, if you make $24,000 your first year part-time and the government wants it's usual third, you face an $8,000 tax bill. Be prepared. Put a third of your income away. (Deductions help, but that $8,000 tax bill includes what's now a 15% Self-Employment tax, which is what you are paying into Social Security.)

In your second year, your quarterly estimated taxes will be based on what you made the first year. Which is another problem, because your first quarterly taxes of $2,000 (a fourth of the $8,000) will be due at the same time you are trying to pay your huge first-year tax bill.

Know that the IRS, as usual, will get you coming and going.

SEASONAL PLANNING

Remember how you took all those Client Cards and threw them into a box because you were done with them. They guided you through all the jobs that first year and were used to make sure you got paid.

It's now the off-season -- winter, or just before you start up your second year. It's time to organize those cards to establish your client base and begin going after repeat and biannual customers.

In the first year, the focus was on creating as many cards and new customers as possible. In the second year and thereafter, the focus is now on repeat customers and selling twice-a-year aeration.

The first thing is to sort the cards alphabetically. Then I take one of the two reduced copies of deposited checks, cut out each check and staple it onto the Client Card for that customer. It's also a good time

ADMINISTRATION

to check the spelling of the name, the address, the phone numbers, and make sure the card matches the check.

Here's why I do that: I had a customer swear up and down I charged him $50 for his yard the previous year. My copy of his $60 check attached to the Client Card prevented an argument. The card tells me what I did and the check tells me what he paid for it.

Next, I take all the cards and sort them by areas (cities, suburbs, whatever is natural). I put them back in the Client Card box, with dividers for each area. Behind them are dividers for each month and for next year.

As I start back to work in March, I pull up the cards in the area I plan to work next and begin calling my old customers there.

If the customer says to call back next month, I slip the card back into the April divider. If he says next year, I slip it behind that divider. If I get no interest at all, I try to get the customer to take down my phone number, but I put the card in my inactive box. I'm not interested in this customer any more.

You use the same system for biannual customers. You take all your March jobs done, paper clip them together, and put them in your September flap. Same with April, etc. Then in September you begin calling all those March customers and telling them it's time to aerate again.

The result for me, working this business part-time now, is that I spend March-June doing repeat customers, promote heavily for new customers the next few months, then fall back on biannual aerations in October-November.

The keys to making this work are heavy promotion for new customers the first year and doing quality aeration jobs that show results. Developing your turf expertise and being available at night to answer questions just increases the customer's commitment to your service -- even if you do charge more.

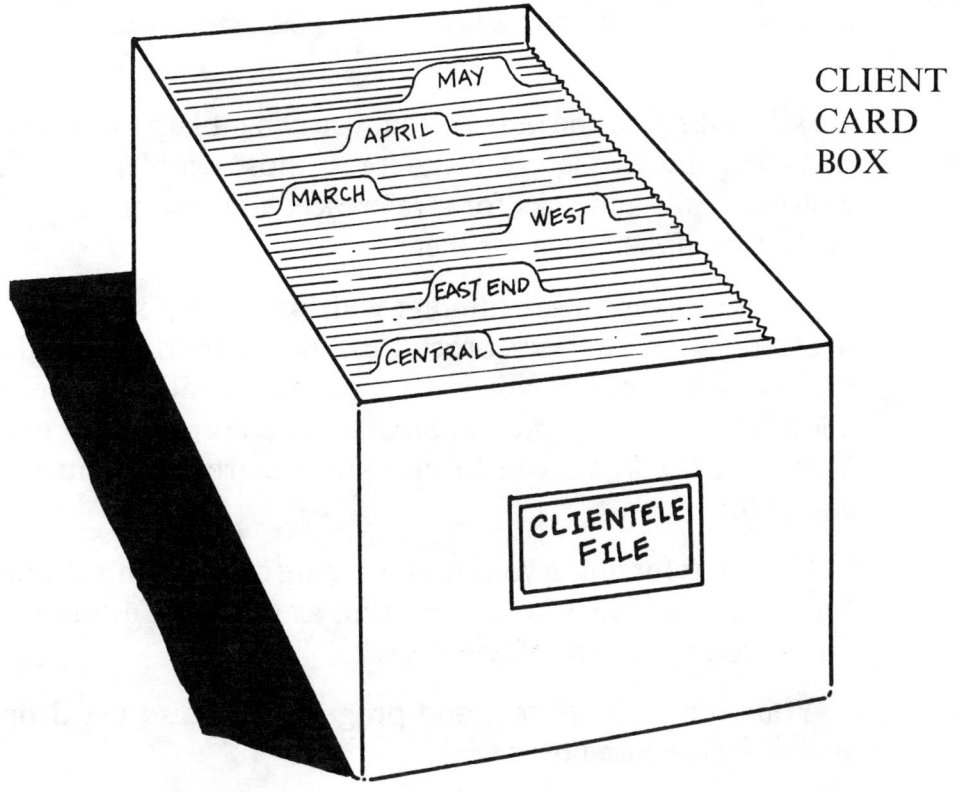

CLIENT CARD BOX

A COMPUTER

All this takes time and after you have established a few hundred clients, you might want to consider computerizing your recordkeeping system. The main purpose of a computer would be to speed up all the shuffling and organizing you have to do with the Client Cards.

If you already love computers, you might do this early. But as a strictly business investment, I would say you have to be in your second or third year, with some 400 repeat customers, before it's worth the cost.

Some guidelines: Don't get a computer with less than 40 megabytes of memory. That's minimum. You need enough memory to sort your mailing list database and to manipulate your bookkeeping database. There are software programs available for small businesses.

Buy a MAILLIST program in which you can sort and arrange your clients by area, zip code, name, or any way you want. Then, when you

ADMINISTRATION

are scheduling for the next season, you can pull up the records from the same neighborhoods and contact just those people. Or, if a potential customer calls and asks for a reference, you can instantly find steady customers in their area for them to contact.

As you become more familiar with your computer, you will be able to create your own flyers, brochures, and other artwork with it. A good word-processing program and a good letter quality or laser printer will allow you to put out professional-looking correspondence every time. You'll eventually be able to save graphic arts expenditures with your computer.

Programs for doing your bookkeeping on the computer are available for as little as $29.95 from such firms as Parsons Technology, who put out a program called MoneyCounts.

Your computer system and programs are also tax deductible and should be expensed over time.

But again, you don't really need a computer for this business. The Client Cards system already outlined will do the job. It's best to think of this as a later reward, because a lot of people do have a lot of fun playing. So look at it that way, not as a necessity.

YOUR START-UP KIT

I've been at this business a long time and to save you time in your start-up phases, I have developed what I call the Pedrotti Start-Up Kit and the Pedrotti Logo Kit.

The Start-Up Kit includes:

- The *Golf Course Green* Pedrotti Bill Card.
- The *Water Savings* Pedrotti Bill Card.
- The Four-picture Aeration Impact Drawing.
- The Aeration Sign.
- Watering Instructions.
- The Envelope Stuffer layout.

These have already been professionally prepared. All you have to do is have your printer substitute your business name and phone number for mine -- and, bang, you are ready to go. Details and price are outlined in Appendix F.

The Logo Kit focuses on using A-1 as your business name and includes:

- The A-1 Lawn Aeration Logo.
- The Envelope Layout.
- The Letterhead Layout.
- The Business Card Layout.

Again, all these have been professionally prepared and the typefaces are indicated so that your printer can match them. The only condition on this -- since there can be only one A-1 per county -- is that you send me a copy of your Fictitious Business Name which shows that you have gotten there first in adopting the name. Details and price on the Logo Kit are covered in Appendix G.

Both of these kits will save you a tremendous amount of time and money in setting the professional image that you want your business to portray. I know because I spent thousands of dollars -- and weeks and months -- going back and forth to the artists and printers trying to get these together the way I wanted them.

I do want you to know I'm planning on making a profit on these. I want you to think of making a profit on everything you do. That's what this book is about.

A FINAL THOUGHT

The major focus in your aeration administration should be to keep on top of costs and always streamline your operation. Always search for labor-saving methods and, even more, time-saving methods.

The goal, always, is to spend as much time aerating and as little time administrating as possible, while still covering all bases.

Answering machines, computers, cordless phones, photocopy machines, and answering devices are better buys than hiring employees. All equipment is depreciable and will pay for itself in the long run.

ADMINISTRATION

SUMMARY

Proper office equipment, tight scheduling, and good record keeping are essential ingredients of any well-run business -- and you are running a business.

A desk, phone lines, a telephone answering device, letterhead stationery, billing invoices, and rubber stamps are early MUSTs. A second phone line, a cordless phone, and a typewriter can come later and will help make your office time more efficient.

Create Client Cards to detail each job and each customer. Use them to plan out the most effective schedule for each day, so that you don't waste time traveling between jobs or in traffic.

Good record keeping habits are essential -- both for tracking customers to recall about an aeration and for getting all the tax breaks possible from the IRS. Be aware that your first year's tax bill can be a crippler if you don't prepare for it.

Streamline your office operations. Look for time-saving devices.

CHAPTER 10

THE BUSINESS SIDE

When you start your lawn aeration service, you will formally become a new small business. This chapter is dedicated to exploring all the in's-and-out's of new businesses you should be aware of.

Starting your own business is not difficult and it does have advantages. A key one is that tax laws like businesses more than they like people. Businesses can deduct goods and services that the average wage earner has to buy with after-tax earnings. When you own a business, much of your spending is tax deductible -- such as the cost of gas/maintenance on your vehicle, part of your mortgage or rent, and utilities.

LEGAL FORMATS

There are three ways to organize your business.

1. Sole Proprietorship
2. Partnership
3. Corporation

Each has its advantages and disadvantages.

You will probably want to begin as a sole proprietor, meaning your business consists of YOU as an individual. You will be responsible for

THE BUSINESS SIDE

all contracts, taxes, liabilities, and accidents. The nice thing is that you are responsible only to yourself.

The down side of being a sole proprietor is that you become liable for any major accidents. This you can handle with insurance (and even more by working very carefully to avoid accidents). Understand that in a business-related legal suit, it's possible for a sole proprietor to lose his home and other possessions.

A sole proprietorship is the easiest way to go. I recommend it.

Avoid partnerships. They tend to get messy. The main legitimate reason for one comes when two people, with differing and complementary skills, contribute equally to a final goal. Aeration doesn't work that way; it's a one-person job. You might be tempted to consider a partnership because you need funding. But that's handled better with a loan. We are not talking about a big capital expenditure here.

Partnerships simply don't have a good track record. People get on each other's nerves. They expect too much from each other. They've ruined many good friendships. One partner will usually end up pulling the weight of another. It strains the relationship. Partnerships may, however, work among compatible family members.

Forming a corporation has a few advantages, but even more disadvantages. As a corporation, your liabilities are limited to the assets of your corporation. You become an employee of the corporation. But incorporating brings along with it more taxes, accounting, payroll taxes, annual meetings with published minutes, and annual registration fees. It costs several hundred dollars. You have better uses for your money. To maximize profit, you need to think small in costs. Stay focused and efficient.

Again, go it alone and stay in control.

NAMING YOUR COMPANY

Pick something short, spiffy, and easy to remember. I chose "A-1" because it got me top billing in Yellow Page directories.

Avoid using your own name in your company name. It suggests a very small company. Looking professional is important in giving customers confidence in your service.

A short name has value of its own; particularly when a homeowner is trying to remember who made his grass green. ANDERSON'S AAA AERATION AND LAWNCARE SERVICES, INCORPORATED, will drive customers up the wall every time they have to call or write a check to you. And can you see that name on your letterhead? So make it SHORT. Long names are a tip off that you're an amateur, not a professional.

FICTITIOUS BUSINESS NAME

One of the first things you should do after picking a name is to file a "Fictitious Business Name" notice. Check with the county. Filing fees are usually between $10 and $20. This also requires placing a classified legal notice in a local newspaper to let the public know that you and your company name are the same. The ad runs about $40.

Call your County Clerk for assistance in getting the paperwork done and to find out where it should be filed. You'll need this paperwork on your company name as proof when opening a business checking account at your local bank, for depositing checks made out to your business.

YOUR ADDRESS

Your place of business should be your home. Don't waste money on commercial space. Again, think small in costs; BIG in profits. You can write off part of your household expenses on your tax return. Talk to your accountant on the percentage you can write off for tax purposes from your mortgage, rent, utilities, etc.

You might think about using a Post Office Box instead of your home address. It depends on how secure you are about being there a long time. (Ownership helps.) The problem is that if you have 1,000 letterheads/envelopes neatly printed and your landlord decides to evict all his tenants, the pretty stationery becomes worthless. If you do move

THE BUSINESS SIDE

often, a postal box has the advantage of providing a consistent business address over a period of years.

If you decide on a Post Office Box, apply for it right away. Some areas have long waiting lists. The cost of the box is tax deductible. Stick with the U.S. Postal Service boxes if they are available. Private postal companies charge a lot more.

PERMITS & LICENSES

If you live in a small town of 80,000 or fewer, and everyone knows everyone, it's good public relations to get whatever licenses and permits the city and county would like you to have. Cities tend to need revenues these days.

In most other areas, I'd say skip it. The problem is that if you live in a major metropolitan area with 10 or 20 or 30 suburban cities, you can thin out your business account quickly paying $40 to $60 a year to each of those cities. You can make money in this business, but there's no point giving away too much of it too fast.

There are no penalties for not having a license, and cities don't have the time or funds to police it. The fees exist solely to give cities revenue. The key thing is that lawn aeration is not a regulated business. Unlike beauticians or pest control companies, you are not using chemicals that do need to be controlled. You're not spreading dangerous pesticides or fungicides (which are regulated). Your products -- the fertilizer and soil conditioner -- are all natural.

INSURANCE

Truck insurance is, of course, vital. You *have* to protect yourself against major damage or injury in case of an accident. But you have to do that whether you are in the aeration business or not. Your truck insurance probably won't cover your equipment.

In protecting yourself against damage to a homeowner's property while on the job, it's more of an open question.

If you do all your own work, if you know that you're careful, if you know you can avoid damage, you might decide not to carry any insurance at all. Many people in the industry don't.

The normal liability issues that come up on the job are when you break sprinkler heads, hit irrigation lines, or damage a fence gate getting to the back yard.

Here's how I handle those: I repair sprinkler heads myself. I tell the customer I don't take responsibility for breaking irrigation lines. (If they were installed by a professional, the lines would be 6" or more deep, well below aeration depth.) Fence damage I fix or get fixed. Worst case might be that you hit a gas main, start a fire, and the house burns down. You just have to calculate the odds on that and decide just how well protected you want to be.

I've been in the aeration business for nine years. In the last three years, I've repaired three sprinkler heads and gotten no complaints about gates or any other problem. (As a side note: It's one advantage of doing your own work. You eliminate anyone else's incompetence or bad decision-making. It also gives you the chance to sell your own expertise on turf problems, which increases the customer's satisfaction with the service he's getting.)

If you have employees, you *do* need liability insurance. No question. Go talk to your agent. A normal commercial policy that covers everything will be around $2,000-$2,500 a year. It's a stiff price, but you can't afford to have someone else dragging you into the poorhouse.

If you do the work yourself, there are other new policies coming on the market today that are a lot more reasonable. Some will protect you from working on someone's property without covering your truck or equipment. They're a lot like major medical; designed to protect you against the big disaster. They cost about $800 a year and I did include a $200 first-quarter payment for one of these in Start-Up Costs as a viable insurance option.

Again, you just have to evaluate how big you feel your risks are and go talk to your agent. Do what you need to feel comfortable.

THE BUSINESS SIDE

FINANCING

The best way to start this business is to have the $6,500 in hand that it takes to buy your equipment, your supplies, and your start-up promotional package -- plus maybe a little more to live on while you are building up your client base in early months.

If you buy all your equipment and supplies up-front, then all the money you make belongs to you.

The rest of this section is here because life is not always quite that convenient. You may have to borrow money to get started.

My best suggestion then is to begin with immediate family. Parents in particular like to see their offspring succeed. If you borrow from family, make the same presentation you would to any other lender. Talk figures, projections, etc. Don't get emotional.

Friends can be a little more deadly. If you do want to try that route, put the loan on a business basis. Write up a contract or promissory note. Make payments as promised. The major benefit of that is: If you can keep their friendship and trust, you will probably have a source of new money the next time you need some. Remember that interest you pay on such loans is tax deductible.

Another source of money is the Small Business Administration (SBA). Check with the people there on what loans are available. (More often, they'll offer you free advice and literature. But that's not bad. Just know it is a resource. They do have counselors who know what the pitfalls are in starting a small business. It's free and worth knowing what they can do for you. Use them as you need to.)

And while we're talking advice and counsel, I'll mention colleges and universities. Many have programs to assist small business start-ups. Usually, it'll be something like getting a senior business major to help you do some special project free -- like, say, you wanted a bookkeeping system. It's a form of on-the-job training the colleges encourage industries to cooperate in. You might see a use for it someplace.

But your major source of financing is likely to be a bank or other major financial institution; at worst, a finance company.

These are some of the common ways for getting money out of them:

- *Credit Cards.* The quickest way to borrow from a bank is to apply for a credit card and take a cash advance for the cash you need. That way you will not have to explain what the money is for. Of course, the interest rate is high. But so is your profit margin. Take that loan pay-off cost into account when you compute your profits.

- *Term Loans.* This is kind of loan you usually get when you buy a car. They are paid back within 36 months or so, at so much a month. You may need collateral, perhaps a second mortgage or your car.

- *Signature Loan.* This runs for a period of months and you pay it off at the due date. Many start-up businessmen apply for such loans, asking for a "vacation" loan and do not refer to their business needs at all. Again, you may need collateral. If you have enough personal property you might be able get the loan on your signature alone.

Banks are tough to get loans from when you have no track record. One way around that is to create what they call "A Business Plan." This is basically a written description of your business and how you expect to make money by doing this and that according to the plan. The plan's major purpose is that banks and lenders love them. I'm not saying you have to do this. If you get the urge, it's one place the SBA and colleges can help you. I point out that this book is *your* business plan.

And remember, don't think small. Larger loans are often easier to get than smaller ones. Don't forget to SHOP. All banks, rates, and penalties are not the same.

Grants might be another funding source, particularly if you are of a minority group. Just keep your eyes/ears open. FREE money is available, but you usually have to search diligently for it.

Other sources of financing include credit unions, retirement plans, the Veterans Administration (if applicable), and the FHA (Farmers Home Administration), which is very liberal in its definition of a "farm community."

THE BUSINESS SIDE

Overall, don't borrow until you need it. The financial cemeteries are filled with people who tried to live too long on credit.

SUMMARY

A sole proprietorship is the best way to start a small one-person business like this. Partnerships and Incorporating are other choices, but they have their disadvantages.

Pick a short business name and file a "Fictitious Business Name" advertising notice in the newspapers as soon as possible.

Investigate business permits, licenses, and insurance; then make your own call on what you want to do about these.

Family can be a good source of funding. Or various types of loans are available from banks, financial institutions, and the SBA.

Don't over-borrow. The business's problems should not last any longer than the business does.

CHAPTER 11

TURF MANAGEMENT

Anyone can buy an aerator and aerate lawns. You can do that and make good money.

You'll make more money though, retain more clients, and receive more referral business when you learn about turf ... when you know what you're talking about. This knowledge eventually separates the amateurs from the professionals in this business.

If you have an opportunity to take courses at a local college or university in turf management, do it. The following will be an introduction to turf management to supplement those courses in higher learning.

The purpose of this chapter is to give you some basic knowledge on lawns ... to get you ready for answering questions customers will be asking ... and to begin the process of making you a turf expert.

The information here is a combination of what I've learned on the job, from taking classes, in discussions with experts, and from lots of reading. If nothing else, this chapter will give you an idea how much there is to learn about turf before you can start considering yourself an expert. This is just the overview. They write encyclopedias about this stuff.

TURF MANAGEMENT

This chapter will cover:
- Anatomy of a Grass
- Cool Season Grasses
- Warm Season Grasses
- Soil Types
- Fertilizer Components
- Soil Conditioner
- Soil pH
- Aeration
- Other Lawn Care Activities
- Fungus and Disease
- Insects

ANATOMY OF A GRASS

A healthy lawn is comprised of thousands of individual grass plants, which in turn are made up of dozens of individual parts.

This section is a quick anatomy lesson on grass parts which will be useful to you as we talk about specific grasses.

Beginning at the top is the grass blade, the most visible part of the plant.

But even more important, at the base of the plant, next to the ground, is what's called the *crown*. It's what the rest of the visible grass grows out of, and as long as the crown isn't damaged, you can cut as many grass blades as you like.

Shooting upward from the crown is the *primary shoot*, which the blades grow out of. There are also other secondary shoots that grow out of the crown. They're called *tillers*. They look just like primary shoots and have leaves growing out of them too. All grasses have these tillers and bunch grasses have a lot of them. It's what makes the lawn grow really thick.

Below the crown are the *roots*, which spread out underground to absorb water and nutrients. They also anchor the plant.

Creeping grasses spread by runners that go along the ground and pop up every now and then to create another grass plant. If runners go under the ground, they're called *rhizomes*. If they go above the ground, they are called *stolons*.

COOL SEASON GRASSES

Cool season grasses are defined as those which grow best below 80 degrees.

These are commonly used in the North, in areas that have snow cover, and high elevations in the south.

These grasses grow actively in the cool weather of spring and fall, and slowly in the summer. While they can tolerate warmth, they cannot survive a severe and intense summer heat.

With ample water, these can remain green year-round and are sometimes seeded over a dormant warm-season grass as a temporary greening substitute during winter months.

The lawns of these grasses are started from seeds -- usually a blend of several kinds. Lawns of a single grass type have the advantage of all the grass looking the same. However, they come with the liability of being wiped out entirely if that one grass gets hit with a disease or pest. That's why grasses are usually sold in blends, with two or three of the grasses eventually taking over the lawn.

The most common cool season grasses are fescue, bentgrass, Kentucky bluegrass and ryegrass.

Both spring and fall are ideal times to aerate cool season grasses.

Now let's take a look at these grasses in detail:

Tall Fescue

Festuca arundinacea

Tall fescue is a very coarse-textured blade of grass. It makes a sturdy lawn than can handle play and other hard usage. It usually stays green all year around.

If you were to pick up a blade of it, you would see parallel veins running vertically up and down. One side is dull, the other side

TURF MANAGEMENT

somewhat shiny. If you were to take it and rub it across the palm of your hand, it would almost feel as though someone were dragging a piece of sandpaper across your palm. Its coarseness is the primary distinction between it and other grasses.

Tall fescue blades are approximately 1/8 to 1/4 inch wide, and it is considered a bunch grass. Wherever you drop a seed is where you get a little individual plant. It does not have the capability of reproducing. When you lose an area in the turf, that area is for all practical purposes dead. It will not rejuvenate by spreading.

This fescue is very drought, disease and insect resistant. It has an extensive rooting system. It can go down to 48 inches deep, so you can see that even if you have an invasion of insects such as grubs, when they start feeding on the rooting system, they can feed on it without signs of stress showing up on the lawn.

Another advantage is that it has a real, dark green textured look when it is treated properly, and that's important when temperatures range as high as 95 to 105 degrees. Most other grasses (except warm season grasses), have a tendency to go into stress at those temperatures. Tall fescue, although it does go into stress at those temperatures, rebounds much quicker, and the plant has less of a tendency to die out. It's one of the best cool-season grasses for transition areas.

In the summertime, you want to develop a canopy in the turf so that it retains its moisture and crowds out the sun from germinating any type of weeds that you might have in your lawn. You ideally want to provide a nice, tall look for your turf so that you can retain moisture -- while keeping weed seeds and insects out of the lawn.

Tall fescue grass should be mowed in the summer at about 2" to 3". Measure your lawn mower height on concrete, not the grass. Measure from the base of the blade to the concrete. You should use a rotary mower on fescue. You cannot use a front reel mower, which is what you traditionally use on a Bermuda grass or a St. Augustine or a Kakuya grass lawn. In the wintertime, you can drop it down to 2-2 1/2". Since tall fescue doesn't develop a thatch, there's no real reason to cut it lower. About the only time you might cut it lower is during reseeding (once every other year), or when the turf starts thinning out.

There are a variety of different ways to overseed the tall fescue yard. To thicken up the turf, pick an appropriate time of the season, either late in the fall or early in the spring. Core aerate the lawn, verticut it, topseed it, and use some peatmoss to top dress it. Obviously, the first thing you want to do is mow the lawn down as low as you can get it.

Primary disadvantages of a tall fescue lawn are its coarse texture, its inability to rejuvenate itself, and its tendency to grow in clumps.

Its carbohydrate reserves are probably more than any other lawn and carbohydrates are essential for the life of a plant, so that, in itself, makes it a very durable, well-conditioned lawn.

A pure strain of fescue has been developed to produce a finer textured blade so you don't end up with that coarseness that some people find objectionable.

One of the more common cultivars (various species; a lot like brand names) is Jaquar. It has good resistance to diseases, heat, drought, wear, and shade.

When you aerate fescue grass, you will thin the grass out at first, but the ultimate result will be wider blades which grow quickly to fill in the thinned areas.

Dwarf Fescue

Dwarf fescue looks very similar to tall fescue, but has a narrower blade and is a little bit finer. You can still see the veins.

Its rooting system will go down to 48 inches, so that it too is very disease and drought resistant. Dwarf fescue can be mowed lower (between 2" to 2 1/4"), not only in the heat but also during the cool season. This is one of its chief benefits. People like a finer blade of grass, and dwarf fescue is very similar in looks to bluegrass.

Like tall fescue, dwarf fescue will be thinned out after aeration but will grow in quickly. Dead spots will have to be reseeded.

TURF MANAGEMENT

Red Fescue

Festuca rubra rubra

Red fescue is often planted with bluegrasses because it blends well and tolerates the shade and dry soils that bluegrass can't. It is considered to be one of the best cool-season grasses for dry areas and shady areas.

Red fescue has a deep green color. It's pretty hardy and can handle acid in the soil well too. The down side is that if fescue gets damaged, it doesn't recover too well. It's also susceptible to summer diseases.

It adapts best to areas where summers are cool, such as mountainous areas and in the Pacific Northwest. Red fescue also works well in large fields where it grows freely without mowing.

Kentucky Bluegrass

Poa pratensis

Kentucky bluegrass is not a bunch grass. It has a very soft and appealing look. If you hold the blade up horizontally, the tip would be in the shape of a boat. One side of the blade is very dull, and the other side is glossy. Bluegrass was predominantly developed for cooler climates.

It has the ability to reproduce at the base through tillers. As those tillers grow horizontally from the plant, they send rhizomes down into the earth and develop a new plant. This characteristic allows it to reproduce and to fill in areas that have been lost to insects or damaged by dog urine.

It is a good grass to grow in sections of the country that have temperatures that range from the 50's up into the 80's. It's good east of the Cascades, the Sierra Nevadas, and the Rockies; also in high elevations of the upper South.

Kentucky bluegrass is easy to grow in these climates, and improved types have stronger resistance to diseases such as strip smut, leaf spot, and summer patch. The seed is inexpensive.

A major drawback to bluegrass is that it's not very heat resistant, even though most textbooks will tell you it is. Once you get up into temperature zones of 85 degrees and more, bluegrass has a tendency to go off-color. It goes into stress, and may die.

It also has problems if mowed too short. The ideal height is 1 1/2" to 3" in the summer. It's also fairly disease prone and improved types usually need greater maintenance, more fertilizer, and more dethatching (usually every two to three years).

The bluegrass root system is not extensive. When you have problems with grubs or web-worms, it shows up easier than in the fescue.

It is, however, a preferred grass because of its texture, color, and uniformity. It's very attractive when the conditions are ideal, a rich, blue-green appearance. Its shade tolerance varies, and the bluegrass has medium to high water and fertilizer needs.

Among popular cultivars are Newport, Eclipse, and Bensun (A-34).

After aeration, bluegrass fills in quickly so it never presents a problem.

Turf Ryegrass

Lolium perenne

Turf ryegrass is a flat grass. It grows about 1/8" wide and is relatively hardy. It can be grown in an area which is going to get a lot of traffic, like walking and playing.

In texture, ryegrass is similar to bluegrass, and most people have difficulty telling them apart. A distinct difference is that ryegrass does not have the boat-shaped tip. If you held bluegrass and ryegrass blades next to each other, and looked at the face of them, then flipped them over, the ryegrass has a greater sheen than the bluegrass does. It has almost a mirror texture from the back side of it.

Ryegrass is often mixed with bluegrass. It is sometimes called a "blue ryegrass." They complement each other because the ryegrass is able to withstand hotter and colder temperatures than the bluegrass.

Ryegrass does have the ability for fast seed germination and establishment. It needs a lot of water, but can tolerate medium shade

TURF MANAGEMENT

and holds up well under traffic. A common use is for overseeding dormant Bermudagrass in the South. It is also used in fescue mixtures.

You have to be careful not to use too much ryegrass in a mixture because it can outmuscle the other grasses and take over. It does work well in the coldest climates and is best suited to coastal areas with mild winters and cool summers.

Ryegrass and bluegrass only root to a depth of about 12" and are susceptible to webworms, grubs, cinchbugs, and other insects.

Turf ryegrass mows cleanly. The best cut is 1" to 2". Common cultivars include Derby and Pennfine.

Like bluegrass, ryegrass fills in quickly after aeration.

Annual Ryegrass

Lolium multiflorum

Annual ryegrass has more disadvantages than advantages.

It does grow fast and hardy -- making a good temporary grass while other grasses are dormant. It's used a lot in the South to fill in when Bermuda goes dormant in the winter.

But annual ryegrass doesn't handle either cold or heat very well, it doesn't mow well and it doesn't like shade much. It only lasts a year anyway and is not recommended as a permanent lawn.

WARM SEASON GRASSES

Warm season grasses are those which grow above 80 degrees and are best suited to the southern part of the United States.

They grow energetically in warm summer months, then become dormant in the winter, often turning brown. These grasses do not do well in cold areas.

Common warm season grasses are Bermuda and St. Augustine.

These lawns are usually grown from stolons, sprigs, plugs or sod. Some are available in seed but seeding doesn't work well. The hybrid

Bermudas and St. Augustine cover quickly with runners. All can crowd out broadleafed weeds.

It is best to aerate these grasses in mid-spring to summer, right after they have their first mowing. The problem with aerating in the cool season when the grass is dormant is that weeds which do grow in cool weather get most of the benefits. That's not usually what the homeowner had in mind.

Let's take a detailed look at some of these grasses.

Hybrid Bermuda

Hybrid Bermuda has the ability to grow just about anywhere ... under the foundations of houses, out into the street, or up through the asphalt. It can become a weed in any flower bed. It is a very aggressive growing grass.

There are not a lot of diseases that will attack it. Probably its biggest problem is that it is very susceptible to grubs. For some reason, grubs prefer this lawn more than any other lawn, and grub damage on the Bermuda grass lawn is very noticeable.

Hybrid Bermuda is a very attractive lawn. Its blade is 1/2" to 1" long, depending on when you mow it, and the grass can handle a temperature range of up to 110-115 degrees. For some reason, warm season grasses seem to do better the hotter it gets.

Hybrid Bermuda propagates from a stolon developed from a base plant. It's a low growing grass and grows across the top of the soil by stolons. It sends rhizomes down. Each of these is an individual plant that has the ability to survive on its own.

It can grow in a soil that is too alkaline or too acidic. It can grow under very adverse conditions. It is a very drought tolerant grass, which means it can go for extended periods of time without any water. When watered, it has the ability to quickly rebound.

It is a popular choice because of its close-croppedness. It can resemble a golf course, and you can cut this grass very short and do some putting. It has a bit higher nitrogen requirement than other grasses do and is very insect and disease resistant. Of all the warm season grasses, it is the best grass to use.

TURF MANAGEMENT

Common Bermudagrass cultivars are Santa Ana, Tidwarf, and Tifgreen.

After aeration, hybrid Bermuda looks very unsightly. Caution people before you aerate a Bermuda lawn. It is going to look as if a pack of dogs has been using their lawn for a toilet. Tell the people the cores will dissolve within a week or so during the watering process. Don't aerate hybrid Bermuda in the winter while it is in its dormant state. It will help bring in weeds.

Common Bermuda

Cynodon dactylon

Common Bermuda grass is different from hybrid Bermuda grass in color and texture. Both spread the same way, but common Bermuda grows vertically while a hybrid Bermuda grass grows horizontally. That is, common tends to grow straight up, while hybrid tends to shoot out to the side.

Because of this vertical growth, you can end up with a yard that has a very sparse, almost unsightly look to it. It requires being cut at 3/4" to 1-1/2". You can't cut it too low because you will take the entire plant off. Conversely, a hybrid Bermuda, growing horizontally with the surface of the soil, helps fill that soil in. The common Bermuda should be mowed with a rotary mower because of that higher cut needed.

On the down side, common Bermuda is very invasive. It will grow a lot of places you don't want it. It does not tolerate shade well. It often turns brown from fall until spring.

Again, common Bermuda looks unsightly right after aeration, until the cores dissolve. It shouldn't be aerated in the winter while it's dormant.

St. Augustine

Stenotaphrum secundatum

St. Augustine grass is a very aggressive-growing grass. A native of the West Indies, it is similar to a Bermuda grass.

It is one of the fast growing grasses, and also one of the best grasses to plant in the shade. Although very heat-resistant and drought-resistant, it does need a lot of water. It will tolerate salty soils, but it won't tolerate lawn traffic as well as other grasses.

A primary difference between this and Bermuda is that St. Augustine has a much coarser blade. The blade is short and wide, with a boat-shaped tip. It has flattened sheaths with prominent mid-veins and a thickened seedhead with embedded spikelets. The spikelets are the seed structure.

The seedheads will grow and spread. Just as Bermuda grass is an aggressive grower when temperatures top 85 degrees, this grass grows fast in hot weather too. It has the ability to withstand temperatures up to 110-115 degrees and as low as 10 degrees.

It is very resistant to diseases and fungus, with the exception of a disease called S.A.D., or St. Augustine Decline. There is no cure for it. The lawn starts going an off-color yellow, the veins become spotted with a blackish substance. It looks very similar to leafspot. When it gets this, all you can do is to cut out that section of the lawn to keep it from spreading, then allow the rest of the lawn to fill that area or put a piece of sod in.

It is also susceptible to chinch bugs and tends to thatch badly. It will need dethatching periodically.

The best mowing height for St. Augustine is 2" to 3". If mowed too low, weeds are likely to gain a foothold and it will suffer from the sun. If mowed too high, thatch tends to build rapidly.

This grass adapts best to the climates of Southern California, Hawaii, mild areas of the Southwest, and Gulf Coast states.

St. Augustine grass does not show dramatic results after aerating but the aeration helps in the long run. If the grass is thick when you aerate, it will be thicker as a result of your aeration process. St. Augustine is generally thicker grass by nature.

Kakuya

Kakuya is African grass that is prominent in Southern California. It was brought into Pacific Beach in the 1900's and has now been spread

TURF MANAGEMENT

throughout the region. Kakuya grass has mostly been propagated through gardeners going from one house to another as they mow lawns.

Kakuya grass grows very tall, as in taller than a house. It is found in creekbeds, and takes on a whole different character if unmowed. It looks like a whole different species, but is actually the same plant.

Kakuya grass doesn't have a wide acceptance. It is not a lawn somebody will go out and choose. It's more likely to arrive by accident than anything else. It grows by rhizomes, is perennial, and has a fringe of fine hairs. If you were to pull the sheath back, you would see hairs protruding from the stem itself. That's one way to distinguish it from St. Augustine.

Kakuya and the St. Augustine have a dormancy zone perhaps as low as 45 degrees, whereas Bermuda grass is higher at about 55 degrees. Bear in mind that it's not the plant above ground that goes into dormancy; that's just a reflection of the rooting system. The soil temperature determines when a plant goes into dormancy.

Like St. Augustine, Kakuya does not show dramatic results after aeration. The improvement in the health of the lawn comes slowly.

SOIL TYPES

It's important to have an understanding about soil because you are going to be working with it on a daily basis.

Soil is basically a lot of mineral particles, mixed with organic matter, air and water. Usually, it is the size of the particles that determine what kind of soil it is.

There are three generic types of soil -- clay, sand, and loam.

Clay

Clay is composed of the smallest mineral particles, so small they are microscopic in size. These tiny particles flatten and fit so closely together that there is very little space between them for air and water.

When clay soils get wet, they dry out slowly because the drainage (the downward movement of water) is hindered. However, the slow drainage helps prevent loss of soil nutrients by leaching.

Many a homeowner will complain about his *oh, so hard* clay soil. But actually, many top soils are made up of clay which has been ground up and padded with other plant nutrients such as mulch or redwood. Eventually, however, this once-loose top soil will slowly compact into the hard clay.

Sand

Sand is at the other end of the scale. It has comparatively large particles that are rounded instead of flattened. The size and shape of the particles provide much more space for air and water.

As a result, sandy soils contain much soil air, drain well, and warm up quickly. They also dry out quickly and the frequent watering that is necessary washes out valuable nutrients.

Decomposed granite is one type of sandy soil.

Loam

Loam covers the ground between the other two -- usually a mixture of clay, silt, and sand particles.

With characteristics between the two, loam is usually considered the ideal soil. It drains well, but doesn't dry out quickly. It contains enough air, water, and nutrients for healthy lawn growth.

SOIL pH

Understanding soil pH at this point is a necessary prelude to understanding fertilizer and soil conditioning in the next sections. So let's do a quick run-though on the pH factor.

The key thing to understand here is that chemical elements and microorganisms in the soil can do a better job of making nutrients available to plants when the soil is nearly neutral rather than too acid or too alkaline.

TURF MANAGEMENT

The pH units measure just how acid or how alkaline the soil is. The letters refer to "potential Hydrogen".

On a pH scale of 1 to 14, 1 is extremely acid and 10 or more extremely alkaline. A pH of 7.0 is neutral. That's the best.

Each unit of difference in pH represents ten times more acidity or alkalinity. For example, a soil with a pH of 4.5 is ten times more acid than a soil of 5.5. Ideally then, maintain a pH range from 6 to 8 and your lawns will do well.

One problem is that if you start adding a lot of fertilizers to a soil that's out of pH balance, then you may be throwing on minerals and elements that are not going to be absorbed by the plant.

(One reason for knowing this is that if your fertilizer doesn't seem to do much good, you might suggest to the customer that he test his soil at the local agricultural extension. Who knows, maybe the pH is out of whack. That gets you and your fertilizer off the hook. Maybe the customer will even be grateful.)

From an aeration point of view, the value of being aware of soil pH is that one of the things you are selling is soil conditioner -- and a major purpose of conditioner is to deal with soil pH.

FERTILIZER COMPONENTS

Fertilizer is one of the most important things to learn about in this business. For one thing, you are going to be selling it.

With the aeration, you will be providing a one-shot fertilization program, and possibly doing it twice a year. This section is designed to give you a basic foundation on the minerals in fertilizer and how they help the plant.

There are roughly 16 minerals or elements that are essential to plant life, much like a balanced diet improves people's health. The ones that we want to concern ourselves with are nitrogen, phosphorus, potassium, magnesium, sulfur, iron, and calcium.

Most of these minerals are found in the structure of the soil. So it's not necessary to add them. But the ones that are usually in the shortest supply in natural soil are nitrogen, phosphorous, and potassium. To be considered to be a complete fertilizer, the mixture must contain these three elements.

The labels on fertilizer bags will tell you just how much nitrogen, phosphorous, and potassium is present. For example, a fertilizer bag might read 25-4-8. This is called the NPK ratio. That means that 25% of the bag content is nitrogen (N), 4% is phosphorous (P), and 8% is potassium (K). Together that totals 37% of bag content. The rest of the fertilizer is comprised of carriers which help the chemicals get to the plant.

Now let's look at the basic components of fertilizer.

Nitrogen

Nitrogen is by far the most important element that plants need and is usually not present in the minute particles of soil. Nitrogen promotes healthy plant growth and gives lawns a healthy color.

Approximately 10% of the nitrogen in plant tissue comes from the atmosphere, and the other 90% from manual application. It is essential in the photosynthesis process for the health of the plant and a vital element in the survival of the plant.

Watering tends to flush nitrogen from the soil. Without nitrogen the lawn stops growing. It becomes pale and yellowish.

Most lawns traditionally require about one pound of nitrogen per growing season, though tall fescue will usually use 4-5 pounds of nitrogen over the course of a year.

At any given time, your lawn can only handle a maximum of one pound of nitrogen per 1,000 square feet. With more than that, there's a chance of burning the lawn. The burning has to do with salt. When you apply fertilizer, you are adding salt to a plant. The salt absorbs all the moisture and that plant is, in a sense, "burned." You create a situation where the lawn may go into a stress condition and it's very difficult for the lawn to recover.

Urea is one form of nitrogen. It is very water soluble. It dissolves immediately.

TURF MANAGEMENT

For cool season grasses (fescue, bluegrass, ryegrass), you need about four pounds of nitrogen per year. The warm season grasses (Bermudas, St. Augustine, Kakuya) need 4 to 8 pounds. But again, not more than one pound at a time.

Phosphorus

Phosphorus stimulates the early formation and strong growth of the roots. It is less important than nitrogen, but still essential.

Basically phosphorus and potassium do the same thing. They help photosynthesis take place. They help the sugars and the enzymes to go from one point in the plant structure to another point.

Phosphorus is needed in high percentages only when the lawn is new and starting to grow. Once established, the lawn needs this in very small quantities.

Because both potassium and phosphorus can only be used in small quantities, it is more cost effective for an aerator to apply fertilizer with ratios which read 46-0-0 or 32-0-0 or 21-0-0. You're only going to fertilize once, right after aerating, so these ratios are the most cost effective.

Potassium

Potassium, or potash, is the second most important fertilizer element after nitrogen. It strengthens lawn grasses and helps them stand up to traffic and resist disease.

Like nitrogen, potassium tends to be flushed out of the soil by watering, but more slowly. It is usually needed in the same quantity as nitrogen. But since the soil does supply some of this, it is not added to fertilizer as heavily as nitrogen.

Magnesium

Magnesium is essential to the development of chlorophyll in the plant tissue. Though important, it is often not added to fertilizer because it is usually adequate in the soil. Magnesium is one of the micro-elements of the soil. To be cost effective, you should never have to apply this trace element.

Sulfur

Sulfur works hand in hand with nitrogen in creating new protoplasm for the plant. It's just as important as nitrogen but is usually abundant enough in the soil. An exception is the high rain areas of the Pacific Northwest, where sulfur is leached away just as quickly as nitrogen is.

Sulfur helps reduce the pH of the soil, by leeching the salt out of the soil mixture. For the most part, soils that are in the pH range above 7.4 or 7.5 are going to need some application of sulfur. Sulfur is traditionally put down twice a year, in early spring and late fall. You generally will not put down any more than 10 pounds of sulfur per thousand square feet. Sulfur is applied all over the country, but it's more aligned with a soil that's alkaline, or very salty.

Iron

Iron darkens the chlorophyll within the structure of the plant and gives the plant a real deep, dark, lush green look. It also can blacken the yard if you overapply it. You can literally turn a yard black. So be cautious about the amount of iron you apply. If a lawn goes black, the grass won't necessarily die, but it does look unsightly.

Ideally, add iron in concentrations of no more than 5%, preferably 2 to 3%. Use iron as a darkening agent along with the nitrogen requirement. Used alone, it could cause a blotchy uneven greening.

Remember that the overall health of the lawn is your goal. You can take a lawn in miserable health, spray it with iron and make it look good. But it's still in miserable health. The greening brought on by the iron application is superficial.

Iron applied to a lawn in stress conditions may only show benefits for a few weeks, while it would aid a heathy lawn for months.

Also remember that when you put a large dose of iron down in a dry season, it could take from four to five months for it to go through the root system. Also, if you put iron on a lawn that isn't watered for two weeks (and the iron bleaches out), it is not going to be absorbed by the plant.

TURF MANAGEMENT

Calcium

Calcium is one of the trace elements, a micro-element that acts like magnesium. It's an aid in developing the rooting system. It helps in developing and storing the carbohydrates, sugars, and starches that the plant tissue needs for survival.

Calcium also is an aid in repairing and stiffening the plant and repairing its wounds. It is usually absorbed through the soil structure rather than from an outside source.

Types of Fertilizers

Walk through a lawn care supplier and you will find a bewildering variety of fertilizers. What's the difference?

A complete fertilizer, again, is one that has the three primary nutrients often missing from the soil -- nitrogen, phosphorus, and potassium. This is your basic mainline lawn fertilizer, separated by brand name and NPK ratio.

Slow release fertilizers are those designed to release their minerals, primarily nitrogen, over a long period of time. The elements are usually encased in a sulfur coating. The coating breaks down slowly and releases the elements slowly.

Liquid fertilizers can be directly added to a tank of water, and are direct, quick release forms of nitrogen to the soil. There's a very high burn potential with water solvent ingredients because they go into nitrate form very quickly -- so you have to follow directions carefully to avoid the burn. These liquid fertilizers are more expensive than other fertilizers and not practical for the large-scale commercial use such as aeration. Green Sweep and Miracle-Gro are good examples.

Organic fertilizers are those whose contents are derived solely from the remains of a once-living organism. For example, manure is an organic fertilizer. In general, these fertilizers also release their nutrients over a slow period of time, but since they rely on soil organisms to break them down, they can't be counted on to release a needed proportion of any one nutrient at the time the plant may need it. With these, you don't have to worry much about burning the plants.

There are other fertilizers that are packaged with insecticides and herbicides. These are designed to prevent weed growth or to kill certain pests. You have to read the directions carefully.

There is a five-step process fertilizers go through in order to be absorbed by plant tissue. Fertilizer can only be used in the form of a nitrate. Some fertilizers bypass four of those steps. For example, ammonium sulfate does and becomes readily available to the plant. When watered, the ammonium sulfate is converted very rapidly and the plant uses it almost instantly. Hence you get that real rapid growth of the plant tissue which contributes to a very heavy thatch layer over a long period of time.

In one growing season, you can increase the thatch layer of a Bermuda grass lawn drastically by using large amounts of ammonia sulfate or ammonia phosphate. Therefore, limit their use. It is better for a turf professional to stick with slow-release products. These stimulate the lawn over a longer period of time. Sulfur-coated products achieve that goal.

If you're not sure you're going to be called back next year, it may be better to use a urea product. That gives you a faster greening effect and can impress people more than a slower-acting regular treatment. A regular treatment program actually does more for a lawn but does it over a much longer period.

SOIL CONDITIONER

There are two basic choices: Either the soil in your area is too alkaline and needs gypsum, or it's too acid and needs lime.

To find what the soil in your area needs, talk to the people who do soil testing. Or check with your local Agricultural Extension.

Gypsum

Gypsum is a soil conditioner. Gypsum interfaces with the soil structure.

TURF MANAGEMENT

It is used predominantly on a clay base soil to act as an interface to break up the molecular structure of the clay. Gypsum adds another molecule to a clay structure. It allows the clay to be freed up and not be so tight.

If you decide to use it as a conditioner, put in about 4% iron. Use a rock gypsum that goes on like a fertilizer so that you don't have a mess with powders that take forever to put down. Fifty pounds of rock gypsum takes about two minutes to put on a lawn. Fifty pounds of powdered gypsum takes a half hour, so you certainly can't offer powdered gypsum or you won't make any money.

You need nitrogen to absorb the iron, so the customer should use a fertilizer such as sulfate of ammonia on a monthly basis for about six months. That will keep the lawn green. A conditioner costs you about $3.00 for a normal 1,000-sq.ft. lawn and I sell it for $12.50.

So if you have a soil that's at 8.5 pH, chances are that plant is doing poorly because it can't get the vital elements to survive. The turf professional needs to start doing sulfur applications to lower that pH value.

Lime

In areas of the country with heavy rainfall, soils are typically acid and lime is applied to neutralize the acid. Grasses grow poorly in acidic soils.

I recommend that you use the newer pelletized lime in these areas. It spreads a great deal faster.

Frankly, I have never used lime in California, so I can't be much help on that. You'll have to check with the turf experts in your area to find out just what they recommend as a soil conditioner in your area and why.

OTHER LAWN CARE ACTIVITIES

Just to make you aware of other lawn care activities that go on in the industry, I will talk about a few.

The purpose here is just to give you some information on these activities so you can talk intelligently to customers about them.

Dethatching

Dethatching is the process of removing that layer of dead and decaying plant tissue that lies between the surface and the green vegetation. The thatch layer hinders lawn growth.

This job is normally done with a dethatching unit or a power rake. A power rake is a piece of turf equipment that mechanically removes thatch with rigid wire tines or steel blades. These blades slice through the turf and lift the thatch debris to the surface for removal.

Dethatch Bermuda grass with a cut machine or a power rake which removes all the dead material that makes up the lawn. Bermuda grass yards accumulate a real heavy matting of dead material that is inherent in this type of lawn. It needs to be raked out in order to encourage proper development and proper growth of grass in the spring.

Dethatching should only be done in the early spring before the temperature gets up to around 55 degrees. This stimulates Bermuda grass coming out of dormancy. You can never take too much out when you dethatch a Bermuda lawn. You can take a lawn right down to the dirt and that is ideally where you want it.

Mow the yard down as low as your front wheel mower can take it. Then dethatch in one direction, rake it up, dethatch it perpendicular to the direction you just dethatch it, rake it up, and continue in this manner, going over the lawn 4 or 5 times.

St. Augustine grass is a different story. Do not dethatch St. Augustine to the degree you dethatch a Bermuda grass yard. The same is true of a kakuya grass yard. It does not require dethatching to the degree that you dethatch a Bermuda grass yard.

Ideally, mow with a front wheel mower down as low as you can get it. But you don't want to remove all the kakuya grass or the St. Augustine. Otherwise it takes forever to come back.

Handle common Bermuda like a fescue yard. Shave it as low as you could get it, aerate it, verticut it, overseed it with common Bermuda grass, top dress it and away you go.

TURF MANAGEMENT

A distinction should be made between annual rye and perennial rye. Perennial rye is used in the blue grass mixes. The annual rye is used to overseed lawns in the winter. Technically, the rye grass is only supposed to come up once a year. But it can rejuvenate itself. Once you start overseeing a lawn with annual rye, you have to continue doing it or it will become a weed. You can't oscillate back and forth. In the springtime, when Bermuda comes out of its dormancy, it's supposed to choke out the rye grass. But a lot of times the rye won't stop until the end of the summer.

Mowers

There are two mainstream types of mowers: The reel mower, the kind most of us used to push around as kids, and the power rotary mower, the one dad bought when we left home and he had to start taking care of the lawn himself.

After that, it's simply a question of whether the horsepower comes from you or from a small engine; whether you want to do the job standing up or sitting down; and whether you want to rake leaves or catch them in a trailing.

Which mower works best depends on the kind of grass and the kind of lawn. Bentgrass, Bermudas, zoysiagrass, and centipedegrass will take a low mow, while bahiagrass, fescues, St. Augustine and bluegrass need a higher cut.

The basic mower list includes:

- *Push Reel Mowers* were once the only home mowers and they are still quite useful on a small lawn. They cut grass low and cleanly if blades are sharp. These are ideal for bentgrass and Bermudas. They are also quieter and the least expensive of mowers. If you don't mind getting a little fresh air exercise with your gardening, they can be a good choice.

- *Power Reel Mowers* give a tailored grass cut, low to the ground. Again, ideal for bentgrass and Bermudas. It's a much crisper, cleaner cut than rotaries and they can deal with land contours better than rotaries. However, they're not practical for rough ground and not a good choice for grasses that need a high cut, such as bluegrass and St. Augustine.

- *Power Rotary Mowers* are the most popular because they maneuver so easily and the motor does most of the work. Its blades cut like a whirling scythe, which makes it perfect for high-cut grasses and weeds. It usually costs less than the power reel mowers, and is much easier to maintain. Few will mow lower than 1" and if set low, will often run into bumps in the lawn. But it is the easy choice for tall growing and less extensively maintained lawns.

- *Riding Mowers* are the choice for large lawns that could take you all day to mow by hand. They come in either reel or rotary models and are obviously the most expensive. They even have models that ride on a cushion of air instead of wheels; greater for smooth lawns but they slide on rough and slope grounds. The thing to remember about these is that they may make mowing fun, but they are not toys for children to play with.

Watering

As you develop your role as a lawn care expert, customers will probably ask you more about watering than any subject except aeration itself.

There's a simple answer: You water when the lawn needs it. No joke. That's as close to the truth as it gets.

How do you know it needs it? Well, it needs it when the soil begins to dry and before the grass wilts. It needs it when the grass starts to lose its bounce-back resiliency. It needs it when lawn color appears to change from bright green to a duller or smoky green. (What's happening is that you are seeing the duller bottoms of the blades because they turn over when they wilt.)

These are all signs of a drying lawn. You can also buy soil moisture testers and coring tubes which you can stick in the lawn and find just how much moisture is in there.

There are a couple of things to watch: Don't mistake dormancy for drying out; grasses also change color when they go dormant in the non-growing season. Don't get too focused on how dry the surface of

TURF MANAGEMENT

the soil is. Much of the time you want the top inches dry and the grass roots having to reach down for deeper water.

As a general rule, recognize that your average lawn needs about 1" to 2" of water a week. You can even measure that by putting out a container and seeing how full it gets.

Be aware that different grasses require different amounts of water. Bluegrass, bentgrass, ryegrass, dichondra, and St. Augustine need high amounts of water. The fescues need less if watered deep. The Bermudas need the least of all.

The real trick to keep the grass roots growing deeply is to wet the soil to a depth of 6" to 8". That takes about an inch of water and lasts about three days. You can stick a screwdriver in it to test how deep the water went (best done about 12 hours later). Then you don't worry about how dry the top is because you want the roots to dig deep for the water.

Early morning is the best time to water. There isn't as much wind and sun evaporation that way. (And, besides, the water pressure is usually better.) Watering at night also beats the evaporation process, but also increases the chance of encouraging fungus. Daytime watering comes with the most evaporation problems. With all that said, never forget the main guiding rule: Water when it works best for you. That's what most people have to do anyway.

Before an aeration, you want the homeowner to water 10 minutes the night before, wait an hour, then water 10 minutes more. That should get the ground moist enough to penetrate the next day, but not make it too muddy to work.

Renovation

Renovation means restoring an established lawn that has been damaged by neglect or mismanagement. It usually means reseeding it or dethatching, which is the process where you're lifting up the dead grass out of the soil. The tall fescue does not develop much of a thatch layer, so normally you wouldn't have to dethatch it. Only if a fescue lawn died off completely would dethatching help lift off the old grass.

A good place to start is to mow the lawn as short as you can possibly get it. Set your mower on the lowest setting. Then aerate the yard thoroughly. Then verticut the yard to break up the cores because you want to deposit them back into the soil as quickly as possible. Then topseed it. Use approximately 10 to 15 pounds of a good quality turf-type tall fescue seed per 1000 square feet. Use one half of your batch in one direction and one half in the opposite direction. Aerating gives the seed a lodging place where it's not going to be subjected to a lot of heat from the day. The best time to renovate is in the early spring or the late fall. Never do it in the middle of summer. In warmer climates it can be done in the winter as well.

The next step is to top dress with steer manure. Don't fall into the trap of using cheap mulches. You're doing yourself a disservice if you attempt to save yourself a few bucks by using crushed bark or the regurgitated telephone pole material on the market. Use steer manure. It has a great thermo capability. That means it has the ability to retain heat and retain moisture. Both aid proper germination of the seed. Once you dress it with steer manure, you roll it in one direction with a roller about half full of water. Then roll it perpendicular to that direction. This gives you good seed-to-earth contact. Never let the seed bed dry out, but don't flood it either. Apply enough moisture to keep the steer manure damp. The germination process takes place when there's an adequate amount of moisture and an adequate amount of warmth. Plan your job in warm weather, and when rains are not predicted, to avoid losing large amounts of seed to flooding.

With fescue, you might want to do this process every other year because this grass does naturally die and thin out. If you have a service, a comprehensive weed and fertilizing package, then chances are you don't have to go through this process.

This is an expensive proposition. It's very labor intensive and a good quality seed is going to cost from $1.70 to $2.70 per pound. So if you have a thousand square feet, and you're going to be using 10 pounds, you're looking at substantial costs in seed alone.

The renovation process for Kentucky blue grass, dwarf fescue, blue rye is the same. Mow it short, aerate it, verticut it, seed it, top dress it, and make sure it's watered properly.

TURF MANAGEMENT

Hybrid Bermuda promulgates by cleaning out the weeds in the area that is going to be transplanted. Dig a void in the ground and plant a hybrid Bermuda sprig. Another method is to broadcast. Take your sprigs and put them into a spreader and cast them about on the ground. Then drop peat moss over the top, roll it into the ground and water it. Some of it takes and some of it doesn't. It's a hit-and-miss method. Rake off the ones that don't grow and get rid of them.

WEEDS

Weeds are as much a part of the lawn scene as the weather. Like the U.S. Mail, neither rain, nor sleet, nor dead of night will stay the weeds from their appointed rounds.

Sometimes it seems like the only way you tell it's a weed is that it's the plant still growing green while everything else needs to be taken care of.

Actually, the best definition I've heard is that a weed is a plant growing in the wrong place. Even the best lawn seed in the world is a weed if it is growing in the flower beds.

The problem with weeds is that they compete with grass plants for water, nutrients, and space. The best defense here is a good offense. If a lawn is healthy and vibrant, it can fight its own way past the weeds.

Controlling weeds basically consists of either preventing them in the first place or destroying them once they appear.

The best prevention is to get rid of as many weeds as possible before planting a lawn. Then you don't have to deal with them later.

Once growing, the best treatment is a post-emergence herbicide such as 1,4-D or 2,4-DP -- both of which are good at controlling the difficult-to-kill broadleaf weeds.

The weeds I'm going to target in this book are:

- *Crabgrass.* A thin-leaf summer weed which begins in early spring and grows fast until early fall. It generally looks like an overgrown, shaggy grass. It's an annual weed, which means it only lives one year. But it reproduces like crazy too.

- *Oxalis.* A big-leaf perennial (lives two or more years) weed that looks something like a four-leaf clover. Its fast growth season is from spring to late summer.

- *Spotted Spurge.* A wide-leaf annual weed that somehow reminds me of an octopus. It has long, visible, reddish branches which spread out over the ground, and the leaves sprout from the branches. Its most aggressive growth is from late spring to early fall.

The best way to keep weeds out of lawns is to have a healthy lawn to begin with -- which means mowing at the right height, watering properly, aerating regularly, and fertilizing at the right time (i.e., not when the grass is dormant and weeds get most of the benefit)

INSECTS

Insects in the lawn are part of the natural order of things. Most do little damage. Some, like fleas, are annoying to people and pets, but no problem for the lawn itself. Many are even helpful.

Yet there are also a few pests such as grubs that can destroy a lawn in no time at all. Grubs are one of the most likely to become obvious while you are aerating. What happens is that whole patches of lawn may come up in aerating, like rolling back a carpet, and you'll see the grubs. These are actually the larvae of different kinds of beetles. They look like whitish worms.

If you see these and notify the homeowner, you might mention that in treatment the entire area of the lawn should be removed so that the insecticide can get into the ground with repeated watering.

One of the most effective insecticides for grubs is diazinon. Once in the soil, it will protect against other lawn pests for up to six weeks.

TURF MANAGEMENT

DISEASES

Spotting plant diseases in lawns can be difficult because it's often hard to distinguish them from all the other things that can be going wrong -- i.e., a brown spot is a brown spot is a brown spot.

That brown spot could be caused by insects. It could be caused by bad drainage. It could be caused by improper watering or mowing. It could be caused by compaction. It could be caused by excessive thatch (the highest probability). It could even be caused by the herbicide that is busy trying to solve some other problem.

Or it could be caused by a bacterial, virus, or fungus disease.

One of the lessons here is that lawn diseases are usually easier to prevent than to diagnose. One of the best ways to prevent disease is to have a healthy, well-cared-for lawn. Which brings us back to lawn aeration -- which is one of the regular maintenance activities that contribute to the development of a healthy lawn.

But for the record, let's take a look at some of the more common diseases you should be aware of:

- *Brown Patch.* Occurs in late summer and is recognized by huge, irregular brown patches. The patches can be up to several feet big. The edges almost look like they've been soaked with water as if the water is trying to get in and the patch won't let it. Attacks Bermudas, fescues, dichondra, ryegrass, zoysiagrass, and St. Augustine. You don't want to fertilize this stuff. There are many lawn chemicals to prevent and control this.

- *Dollar Spot.* Occurs from spring through fall and is recognized by small beige-colored spots that may be anywhere from one inch to a foot in size. Or a lot of them can come together and make one giant patch. This fungus disease attacks bentgrass, Bermudas, fescues, bluegrass, and ryegrass, particularly those that haven't been fertilized enough. You attack it by increasing the fertilizer, taking out thatch, and watering well. There are also many chemical controls.

- *Fairy Ring.* Occurs from spring through fall and is recognized by rings of dark green grass that seem to surround drying grass. It's a fungus disease and the grass in the center is dying because water isn't able to get into the soil. This attacks all grasses. This is one disease that's hard to get rid of unless you want to dig up the whole area and replant. You can try to improve the dying center with more fertilizer, aeration, and watering; but mostly, you just get used to it. There aren't many chemical controls that knock this thing out.

- *Leaf Spot.* Occurs from spring through fall and is recognized by odd-shaped brown patches with a dark, blackish edge. You can even see this stuff on the grass blade. This disease attacks Bermudas, fescues, and bluegrass. Controls include giving the area more light (by, say, trimming away tree branches). Aeration is good for this too, because it opens up the area and allows more water into the soil. There are also many chemical controls.

- *Pythium Blight.* Occurs in late summer and tends to favor newly growing lawns (though it can attack others). It's recognized by irregular brownish patches that can be anywhere from a few inches to several feet in diameter. If you look at the darkish grass on the patch edges on a damp morning, you can see this somewhat grayish fungus on the blades. This disease attacks Bermudas, bluegrass, fescues, and ryegrass. This flourishes when it's hot and moist. So don't overwater when it's hot. There are also several chemical controls.

- *Rust.* Occurs from late summer to fall and is recognized because it creates rust-colored patches. If you look at the grass blades, it looks like someone scattered rust-dust on them. Rust attacks nearly all grasses but doesn't damage the grass much. (It just makes your lawn a different color than your neighbor's.) To control it, feed the grass a lot of fertilizer to make it grow fast, then cut it every couple of days. You don't usually get into the chemical controls on this unless it's really bad.

Again, the best way to deal with diseases is to avoid them with a healthy lawn. That means picking the right seed for the climate, mowing at the proper height, fertilizing properly, watering deeply when the grass needs it, dethatching regularly, and aerating regularly.

TURF MANAGEMENT

SUMMARY

Obviously this chapter is a broad view of a number of distinct subjects. Use it to begin your business, but if you expect to continue and develop a professional approach to this business, further education in turf management is essential.

Like all chapters in this book, the goal here has been to put you on the road toward a thriving profitable business.

In Start-Up costs, Promotion, Selling, Administration, and so on, I was able to give you all the tools needed to begin making money quickly. So go get it! The market is there, the money is there, and the information in this book will put you many steps ahead of your competitors.

But remember that one of the themes in this book has been to do a quality job and to know more about lawn care than your competitors. And this chapter, more than the others, is just a starting point.

You will have to ask questions, and learn about the soils and grasses in your particular area. It will take some work. Just know that the more you learn about lawn care, the more money you will make -- because the customers will want you to come back.

And the nice thing is that they are willing to pay you for it.

A FINAL WORD

I'd like to take a moment to thank you for reading this book.

What I feel good about now that I've finished this book is that it's honest. There are obviously products and approaches I favor from my experience, but I've left it up to you by giving you all the choices. All I wanted to do when I started this was to pass on what I've developed and how it's worked for me. I think I've done that. There's nothing bogus here. The market is rapidly expanding and I've given you all the tools you need to capitalize on it.

I've read my own share of opportunity magazines and self-help books. I know how annoying it is to shuffle through the information and discover that all you've got is a lot of farfetched, empty promises. This book has no empty promises. Period.

I know, from being in your shoes, that good opportunities are hard to find. I hope this is the right one for you. **Great Luck .... I wish you big bucks.**

APPENDIX GUIDE

The following is an outline of what the various appendixes cover:

APPENDIX A   **Homeowner Letter** . . . *This is the cover letter to the information packet which I give each customer after the job.*

APPENDIX B   **Watering Instructions I** . . . *This is the one-page watering instructions I leave for those customers where I don't fertilize because a gardener or lawn care service is already doing that.*

APPENDIX C   **Watering Instructions II** . . . *These are the watering instructions I leave for those customers where I do fertilize and usually add soil conditioner.*

APPENDIX D   **Turf Tips** . . . *This provides tips to the customer on how to take care of his grass. It helps to establish that I am an expert and can help the customer with his lawn.*

APPENDIX E   **Turf Facts** . . . *Another little bonus that indicates you're paying attention to knowing about lawns and helps leave the impression that you are an expert in providing their service.*

APPENDIX F   **Pedrotti Start-up Kit** . . . *A compilation of promotional tools I've developed over the years which will be useful to you in providing a quick start-up. Includes a list and cost.*

APPENDIX G   **Pedrotti Logo Kit** . . . *A similar compilation of logo tools I've developed over the years. They can save you a lot of time getting started. Includes a list and cost.*

APPENDIX H   **Sources** . . . *Names, addresses, and phone numbers which may be helpful to you and a description of how they may be useful in establishing your business.*

APPENDIX I   **Publications** . . . *A list of books and magazines which will increase your lawn knowledge and broaden your business, sales, organization, and promotional skills.* Plus many more money-making ideas in other areas.

HOMEOWNER LETTER

YOUR LOGO...

Thank you for employing my firm for your turf aeration needs. I can assure you that we offer the highest quality aeration service available anywhere. It has been our pleasure working on your property.

Enclosed you will find literature regarding aeration and watering. Please be sure to read the watering instructions as they are very important. Because San Diego's soil base is extremely compacted, we recommend aeration twice a year, once in the spring and again in the fall.

If you have any questions about lawn care or need a referral for a gardener or possibly the purchase of a new lawn mower or mower service, please don't hesitate to call me. Servicing you is my pleasure.

Thank you again for your business. If you are happy with our service, please tell your friends. Your referrals are very important to us. If for some reason, you are not completely satisfied with our service, please call and let us know how we may correct any problem.

Your Name
Resident Turf Manager

(You do this on letterhead stationary which includes your logo, address, and phone number.)

WATERING INSTRUCTIONS I

IMPORTANT INFORMATION:

WATERING INSTRUCTIONS

Robin Pedrotti
Resident Turf Manager
A-1 LAWN AERATION
(619) 571-2884

Now that your lawn has been aerated, its watering requirements need to be adjusted in order to reduce your watering bill.

You have wisely employed a professional lawn care company to treat your lawn. You do not need to do any special watering after aeration. In fact, it is best that you allow the lawn to dry out and absorb oxygen. Many people do not realize how important oxygen is to a lawn.

It is important to realize that your lawn will need water *only* when the soil is completely dry. If you insert your finger into an aeration hole and the soil is still moist, it is too soon to water.

If, before aeration, you watered your lawn daily, you should be able to decrease your watering to two deep soakings a week. For water efficiency, we suggest watering twice in the morning. For example, if you currently water for 20 minutes on each valve at 6:00 a.m., re-program your clock to water for 10 minutes at 6:00 a.m. and again for 10 minutes at 7:00 a.m. This allows for the water to soak in, thereby reducing runoff.

The goal here is to water the least amount without causing damage to the turf. How much? Well, this depends on your soil conditions, the weather, and the type of grass that you have. The cool season grasses such as fescue and bluegrass need more water than the warm season grasses such as Bermuda, St. Augustine and kakuya. As a rule of thumb, watering can be cut back to 2 deep soaks, twice a week. Many Bermuda lawns require only one deep soak a week. **CAUTION:** If your lawn develops dry spots, increase watering to avoid damage.

If any of the above information conflicts with any special instructions you received for your particular type of grass, please follow your lawn care company's advice.

WATERING INSTRUCTIONS II

IMPORTANT INFORMATION:

WATERING INSTRUCTIONS

Robin Pedrotti
Resident Turf Manager
A-1 LAWN AERATION
(619) 571-2884

Now that your lawn has been aerated, its watering requirements need to be adjusted; first, to avoid fertilizer burn, and secondly, to reduce your watering bill. If you ordered regular service with the free fertilizer, please follow the "A" instructions below. If you ordered service with the soil conditioning treatment, as most customers do, please follow the "B" instructions.

A

Instructions for Service with Regular Fertilizer.

Make certain to deep soak your lawn as soon as you can after service, preferably on the same day. Soak your lawn 2 times for approximately 15 minutes each time. This will break down the fertilizer into a water soluble form so that it may enter the root zone.

You may cut back on your watering immediately after the fertilizer is soaked into the ground. Our recommendation is to continue watering heavily (once a day for 12-15 min.) to induce the erosion process of the cores so that they are broken up by your lawn mower blade easily. In either case, allow a minimum of 10 days after service (preferably 14 days) before mowing your lawn. This will allow the cores to break up and add bacteria to the soil, which will naturally reduce thatch build-up.

After the first mowing, you may dramatically reduce your watering cycle. This is important because, as my advertisement states, you will save at least 60% on your watering time and costs. In order to accomplish this, you cannot go back to your original watering practices or no savings will be realized. We recommend watering at least 2 times each week.

The goal here is to water the least amount without causing damage to the turf. How much? Well, this depends on your soil conditions, the weather, and the type of grass that you have. The cool season grasses such as fescue and bluegrass need more water than the warm season grasses such as Bermuda, St. Augustine and kakuya. As a rule of thumb, watering can be cut back to 2 deep soaks, twice a week. Many Bermuda lawns require only one deep soak a week. **CAUTION:** If your lawn develops dry spots, increase watering to avoid damage.

WATERING INSTRUCTIONS II

B

Instructions for Service with Soil Conditioning

Your lawn has received the best service possible. The extra expense in the soil conditioner will have a very positive impact on your lawn over the next six months. It will neutralize the soil Ph via leaching out salt damage and continuing to loosen the hard soil. This process is recommended along with aeration twice a year.

Deep soak your lawn 2 times a day for a period of 12-15 minutes for 2 continuous days after service. <u>Do not mow the turf for at least 10 days after service</u>. If turf is mowed before this period, a portion of the soil conditioner will be picked up by the mower. Although this process uses a lot of water in the beginning, the soil conditioner needs to be broken down from its pelletized form. At the same time the cores are broken down so that the first mowing after service will be easily accomplished.

After the first mowing, you may dramatically reduce your watering cycle. This is important because, as my advertisement states, you will save at least 60% on your watering time and costs. In order to accomplish this, you cannot go back to your original watering practices or no savings will be realized. We recommend watering at least 2 times each week.

The goal here is to water the least amount without causing damage to the turf. How much? Well, this depends on your soil conditions, the weather, and the type of grass that you have. The cool season grasses such as fescue and bluegrass need more water than the warm season grasses such as Bermuda, St. Augustine and kakuya. As a rule of thumb, watering can be cut back to 2 deep soaks, twice a week. Many Bermuda lawns require only one deep soak a week. **CAUTION:** If your lawn develops dry spots, increase watering to avoid damage.

TURF TIPS

TURF TIPS

* Water only in the cool of the day to reduce evaporation. Mornings are best.

* Give special attention to "hot spots" in your lawn that dry out quickly.

* During the warm season, turf grass such as fescues and blue grass should have a high mowing setting in hot weather. This slows down evaporation and increases water retention in the plant.

* Water deeply. Soaking the soil to approximately 6" forces the roots to reach for moisture, thus increasing the turf's drought resistance and watering requirements. Do this by watering for 10 minutes 2 times in the morning. Allow one hour in between watering cycles to allow for water absorption into the soil, which will reduce water run off and waste. Then allow soil to completely dry out before watering again. It also reduces the risk of a fungus.

* **Never** water in the evening. This will invite fungus to your turf.

* Talk to your neighbors with lawn experience and learn to identify a lawn with a fungus. From July through mid-September, many fescues are attacked by a fungus which appears as a dead spot. The only solution is to spray the entire turf area with a fungicide. Ask your nurseryman for assistance or call us.

TURF FACTS

TURF FACTS

Did you know.....?   A lawn that is only 50'x50' cleans enough air and produces enough oxygen to provide a family of four with all the clean fresh air the family needs.

The human body is about 50% water by weight, but typical grass plants are between 75% and 85% water. Reducing water 10% can sometimes cause the death of individual grass plants.

The total turfgrass area in the United State is estimated at 25-30 million acres -- about the size of five New England states. A little over 80% of this is lawns.

Grass plants trap much of the 12 million pounds of dirt and dust released annually into the atmosphere. (That's why airport runways are separated by grassy fields.)

The three primary mineral elements necessary to comprise a complete fertilizer for lawn growth are Nitrogen (N), Phosphorus (P), and Potassium (K). Want to know the percentage of each in a fertilizer bag? Look for them by their uptown names: N, P_2O_5, & K_2O.

In 50's jargon, Grass is *cool* -- namely, about 30 degrees cooler than asphalt and 10-14 degrees cooler than bare soil.

Undesirable noise levels can be reduced 20 to 30 percent by grass areas that absorb sounds.

A healthy lawn absorbs rainfall six times more effectively than a wheat field -- and four times better than a hay field.

Setting your mower higher in hot weather can slow down evporation of water.

PEDROTTI START-UP KIT

I promised to make life easier for you and now I am going to detail what I've included in my Start-Up kit. It costs $79.00.

This is designed to save you all those hours of trooping back and forth between artists and printers that I spent. It also saves hundreds of dollars -- for me, it was thousands because I worked hard to get these just right -- that you will have to spend to get the graphic designs that make the statement that this is a professional company the homeowner is dealing with.

The Start-Up Kit includes:

- The *Golf Course Green Pedrotti Bill Card*.......*See Page 77*
- The *Water Savings Pedrotti Bill Card*..........*See Page 69*
- The Four-picture Aeration Impact drawing......*See Page 11*
  THIS VISUAL SELLS JOBS !
- The Aeration Sign.........................*See Page 87*
- The Envelope Stuffer Layout..................*See Page 73*
- Watering Instructions......................*In Appendix*

As I mentioned, these have already been professionally prepared. All you have to do is have your printer substitute your business name and phone number for mine.

To order, send $89.00 to Prego Press, P.O. Box 23945, San Diego, CA, 92193. (See order forms beginning on page 195.) Allow two to three weeks for delivery.

For overnight delivery, add $35.00, which includes overnight freight.

PEDROTTI LOGO KIT

This offer is focused on those who want to use A-1 Lawn Aeration as a company name. This kit is designed to save you the cost and effort of recreating the same or similar logo art. The Logo Kit costs $89.00.

Since there can only be one A-1 Lawn Aeration company in each county, what I will need from you is a copy of the Fictitious Business Name notice which establishes that you have secured the rights to that name in your county. Remember, this is a business owned by you. That I have one by the same name is purely coincidental.

The Logo Kit includes:

- The A-1 Lawn Aeration Logo. . . . . *See Page 125*
- The Letterhead Layout.
- The Envelope Layout.
- The Business Card Layout.

Again, all of these have already been professional prepared and the typefaces are indicated so that your printer can match them and substitute your own name, address, and phone number.

To order, send **$69.00** to Prego Press, P.O. Box 23945, San Diego, CA, 92193. (See order forms beginning on page 195.) Allow two to three weeks for delivery.

For overnight delivery, add $35.00, which includes overnight freight.

SOURCES

Robin Pedrotti
Prego Press
P.O. Box 23945
San Diego, CA 92193

The author. Would love to hear from you. Send us your success stories. It is very rewarding to hear about your personal accomplishments.

PLCAA
Professional Law Care
Association of America
Suite C-135
1000 Johnson Ferry
Road NE
Marietta, GA
30068-2112
800-458-3466

Established in 1980, the Professional Lawn Care Association of America (commonly known as PLCAA—Plaque-Ah) has become a powerful voice for the lawn care industry. The group provides special services to its members and can advise you on subjects such as risk management and employee training. It also has a monthly newsletter, and is a powerful federal/state lobbying group. The PLCAA logo added to your business demonstrates to your customers that you are a committed lawncare professional.

PUBLICATIONS

BOOKS

TESTED ADVERTISING METHODS
By John Caples (Englewood Cliffs, N.J.: Prentice Hall, 1974) ... *An old book but a great one to get your feet wet in advertising, and one of the first you should read.*

NEGOTIATE TO CLOSE
By Gary Karrass (New York: Simon and Schuster, 1985) ... *Good for learning negotiation skills in selling soil conditioner, aeration, and anything else. Probably the second book you should read.*

WHAT THEY DON'T TEACH YOU AT HARVARD BUSINESS SCHOOL
By Mark H. McCormick *(New York: Bantam Books, 1986) ... Excellent book, excellent author. Strong on time management skills, organizing, selling. Highly recommend it.*

WHAT THEY *STILL* DON'T TEACH YOU AT HARVARD BUSINESS SCHOOL
By Mark H. McCormick (New York: Bantam Books, 1989) ... *More on winning strategies for buying, selling, managing and negotiating. Both books good for developing relationship with your customers.*

IN SEARCH OF EXCELLENCE
By Thomas J. Peters and Robert H. Waterman, Jr. (New York: Harper & Row, 1982) ... *Tells what mega-corporations are doing. Emphasizes stressing quality. Optional and heavier reading, but good food for thought here.*

COMMUNICATING THROUGH LETTERS AND REPORTS
By Wilkinson, Clarke, and Wilkinson (Homewood, Ill.: Richard D. Irwin, Inc., 1983) ... *Good book for learning how to write business letters and how to improve all communications to your customers.*

THE NEW MUTUAL FUND INVESTMENT ADVISOR
By Richard C. Dorf (Chicago: Probus Publishing, 1986) ... *I want you to get used to the idea you are going to be making a lot of money. Here are some ideas for investing it.*

(Magazines on next page)

PUBLICATIONS

MAGAZINES

GROUNDS MAINTENANCE
Published monthly by Intertec Publishing Corp. Circulation: 1-913-541-6633. Mailed free to qualified persons in landscaping design, construction, maintenance, and related fields. Non qualified subscriptions: $30 per year....*A broad view of landscape planning and maintenance.*

LANDSCAPE MANAGEMENT
Published monthly by Edgell Communications, Inc. Circulation: 1 East First St., Duluth, MN, 55802. 1-218-723-9200....*Another good trade magazine.*

LANDSCAPE TRADES (Canada's Premier Horticultural Trade Publication)
Published eleven times a year by the Horticultural Publishing Division of Landscape Ontario Horticultural Trades Association. Circulation: 1293 Matheson Blvd E., Mississauga, Ontario L4W 1R1. 1-416-629-1184. $20 a year in Canada; $30 a year in U.S....*Wide ranging articles from overviews of international landscape design to new products and industry news.*

LAWN AND LANDSCAPE MAINTENANCE
Published monthly by GIE Inc. Circulation: 4012 Bridge Ave., Cleveland, OH, 44113, 1-216-961-4130....*Another good trade magazine.*

PRO
Published bimonthly by Johnson Hill Press, Inc. Circulation: P.O. Box 803, Fort Atkinson, WI, 53538-0803. 1-414-563-6388. $23 per year....*A good business management overview for professionals in lawn maintenance.*

TURF
Published monthly by NEF Publishing Co. Circulation: P.O. Box 391, St. Johnsbury, VT 05819. 1-800-422-7147. $12 per year, $22, two years, $28, three years....*Short, useful articles on current turf maintenance trends with product reviews.*

PUBLICATIONS

OTHER OPPORTUNITIES

Lawn Aeration: Turn Hard Soil Into Cold Cash
by Robin Pedrotti

A part-time business that will bring you as much money working weekends as you earn on your full-time job. Or a career that will keep you and your employees comfortable for years to come. For a business with this kind of appeal to customers and profits for entrepreneurs, you can't start up cheaper or move ahead faster. All you need is your own good motivation and this step-by-step book. It's all here, from your dream of financial independence to the day-by-day tasks that will smooth out the coming seasons of success in this little-known field of lawn care $25

How to Earn $15 to $50 an Hour and more
With a Pickup Truck or Van
by Don Lilly

Unemployed? Underemployed? Don't be at the mercy of employers, economic slumps, job shortages, or skill deficiencies. This work-oriented how-to book leads you through each step necessary to set up your own business. All you need is a pickup truck or van, a few basic tools, and a telephone. Illustrated with line drawings, it includes a rate chart, sample advertising, sample business cards, reproducible artwork...and all the sound advice you need for turning your vehicle into a "Money Machine." $16.95

Pickup Truck Dump Box

ATTENTION PICKUP OWNERS: Would you like to have a load dumping capability for your truck without spending the $1,000-$5,000 for a conventional hydraulic system? This detailed step-by-step instruction booklet shows how—with less than $150 in materials—you can build and install this Pickup Truck dump Box in your truck in one weekend. Judged "Best New Invention" at the SPRING '83 NEW PRODUCTS AND INVENTIONS EXPO in Nashville, Tenn. $11.95

PLUS THESE OTHER MONEY-MAKING REPORTS:

How to Start Your Own Paper Recycling Business	$8.95
How to Make up to $750 Next Weekend	$8.95
How to Make $5000 a Month or More with Garage Sales	$8.95

(See order form following these pages.)

$500 START UP

Start Your Lawn Aeration Business for under $500

There are very few businesses that you can start for less than $10,000. I recommend an investment of about $6,500 for beginning in lawn aeration, and I guarantee that your startup costs can be back in your pocket within months.

Still, there's always a way to juggle hard work, clear thinking and investment dollars—a way to let you begin aerating lawns for less than a $500 initial outlay. You can do it; here are the bare essentials.

Truck You own	
Ryan LA-28 Aerator, including trailer daily rental	$100
Broom	25
Hand-held fertilizer spreader	35
Gloves/Tools	25
Irrigation Flags	5
Fertilizer (1 bag)	18
Telephone Machine	69
Business Cards	20
Rediform Statements	5
Street Map	15
Company Name Typeset	10
Pedrotti Start Up Kit	89
2000 Printed Bill Cards	45
TOTAL	**$461**

SAVE TIME: use this handy form to order

Please print clearly in ink.

_____   _____
Name   Phone (include area code)

_____
Address (include apt number)

_____   _____   _____
City   State   Zip

Title	Quantity	Cost	Total
Law Aeration: Turn Hard Soil Into Cold Cash	_____	$25.00	_____
How to Earn $15 to $50 an Hour and More with a Pickup Truck or Van (Revised Edition)	_____	$16.95	_____
Pickup Truck Dump Box Plans	_____	$11.95	_____
How to Start Your Own Paper Recycling Business (Report)	_____	$ 8.95	_____
How to Make up to $750 Next Weekend (Report)	_____	$ 8.95	_____
How to Make $5000 a Month or More with Garage Sales (Report)	_____	$ 8.95	_____
PEDROTTI START-UP KIT	_____	$89.00	_____
PEDROTTI LOGO KIT	_____	$69.00	_____
		Sub Total	$ _____
		California residents add 7.75% sales tax	$ _____
		Shipping (see below)	$ _____
		Total	$ _____

Shipping Charges: For ground shipments, add $3.50 for the first item and $1.50 for each additional item. Allow two to three weeks for delivery. Canadian residents must add $4.00 for shipping and all payments must be in American dollars. For overnight delivery on the Pedrotti Start-Up Kit and Logo Kits only, send a total of $15.00 which includes overnight freight.

100% SATISFACTION GUARANTEED!
If you are not completely satisfied, you may return any item for a full refund.
(Offer does not include Pedrotti Start-Up/Logo Kits or shipping charges)

Cut and mail this page with check or money order to:
Prego Press   P.O. Box 23945   San Diego CA 92193

PUBLICATIONS 195

Notes

SAVE TIME: use this handy form to order
Please print clearly in ink.

_____   _____
Name   Phone (include area code)

_____
Address (include apt number)

_____   _____   _____
City   State   Zip

Title	Quantity	Cost	Total
Law Aeration: Turn Hard Soil Into Cold Cash	_____	$25.00	_____
How to Earn $15 to $50 an Hour and More with a Pickup Truck or Van (Revised Edition)	_____	$16.95	_____
Pickup Truck Dump Box Plans	_____	$11.95	_____
How to Start Your Own Paper Recycling Business (Report)	_____	$ 8.95	_____
How to Make up to $750 Next Weekend (Report)	_____	$ 8.95	_____
How to Make $5000 a Month or More with Garage Sales (Report)	_____	$ 8.95	_____
PEDROTTI START-UP KIT	_____	$89.00	_____
PEDROTTI LOGO KIT	_____	$69.00	_____
	Sub Total		$ _____
	California residents add 7.75% sales tax		$ _____
	Shipping (see below)		$ _____
	Total		$ _____

Shipping Charges: For ground shipments, add $3.50 for the first item and $1.50 for each additional item. Allow two to three weeks for delivery. Canadian residents must add $4.00 for shipping and all payments must be in American dollars. For overnight delivery on the Pedrotti Start-Up Kit and Logo Kits only, send a total of $15.00 which includes overnight freight.

100% SATISFACTION GUARANTEED!
If you are not completely satisfied, you may return any item for a full refund.
(Offer does not include Pedrotti Start-Up/Logo Kits or shipping charges)

Cut and mail this page with check or money order to:
    Prego Press   P.O. Box 23945   San Diego CA 92193

INDEX

A
Acid soil	161-162
Administration	121-140
Advertising	93
Advertising content	76-80
Air blower	36
Alkaline soil	161-162
Annual ryegrass	156
Answering machine	122
Anti-rust agents	37

B
Bensun	155
Bermuda, common	158
Bermuda, hybrid	157
Bidding	53-63
Billing	126
Brochures	74-75
Brown patch	176
Bulletin boards	85

C
Calcium	166
Card table theory	22
Cards, customer	127, 129-130
Classen Mfg. Co.	28
Clay	160-161
Client cards	127, 129-130
Close	
alternative	103
assumption	103
Ben Franklin	103
puppy dog	104
Closing the sale	103-104
Common Bermuda	158
Compaction	10-11
Computer	137-138
Consultation	61
Core Message	66
Core aeration	10-12
Corporation	141-142
County fairs	95
Crabgrass	174-175
Credit cards	147
Customer cards	127, 129-130
Customers, repeat	115-118

Cyclone B1	35
Cyclone B3	35

D
Decimal pricing	56
Depreciation	134
Dethatching	169
Diseases	176-178
Dollar spot	176
Door Hangers	71-72
Door-to door promotion	81-82
Drainage	14
Dwarf fescue	153

E
Ear protection	37
Envelope Stuffers	72-73
Equipment	25-40, 170-171
Equipment, office	122-124
Expense, home office	134
Expenses, operating	134

F
Fairy ring	177
Fertilizer bin	36
Fertilizer	38, 162-167
Fescue, tall	151-153
Fescue, dwarf	153
Fescue, red	154
Fictitious business name	143
Financing	146-147
Flyers	67, 71-73, 76-80, 109-110
Foot traffic	49
"free"	80
Full-time outlook	23

G
Garden shops	82
Gloves	36
Grasses	151-160
Grasses	
annual ryegrass	156
common Bermuda	158
cool season	151-156
dwarf fescue	153

INDEX

Grasses (continued)
    hybrid bermuda   157-158
    Kakuya   159-160
    Kentucky Bluegrass   154-155
    red fescue   154
    St. Augustine   158-159
    tall fescue   151-153
    turf ryegrass   155
    warm season   156-159
Grease gun   37
Green Machine   36
Grubs   175
Guarantees   80
Gypsum   38, 50, 167-168

H
HiProfit Share   54-55
Home office expense   134
Hybrid Bermuda   157-158

I
Insects   75
Insurance   144-145
Invoices   126
Iron   165
Irrigation flags   37

J
Jacobsen Textron   28

K
Kakuya   159-160
Kentucky bluegrass   154-155

L
Lawns, estate   57-58
Lawns, small   56-57
Leaf spot   177
Licenses   144
Lime   39, 50, 168
Listening   110
Loam   161
Loans, signature   147
Loans, term   147
Logo Kit   139, 189
Logo   124-125, 139

M
Magnesium   164-165
Manure   173
Market Share   53
Motorcycle straps   37
Mowers   170-171

N
Naming your company   142-143
Need, developing   105-106
Newport   155
Nitrogen   163-164

O
Operating expenses   134
Oxalis   175
Oxygen   14

P
Part-time outlook   24
Partnership   141-142
Pedrotti Start-up Kit   138, 188
Pedrotti Logo Kit   139, 189
Pedrotti Bill Card   67-70
Permits   144
Pests   175
Ph, soil   161-162
Phone, cordless   123
Phosphorus   164
Planning, seasonal   135-136
Poor drainage   14
Potassium   164
Price, minimum   56
Pricing   53-63
Pricing, decimal   56
Primary shoot   150
Profit Share   54-55
Promotion distribution   81-88
Promotion   65-96
Promotional gifts   90
Promotional shirts   90
Promptness   99-100
Pythium blight   177

R
Ramp   33

INDEX

Ransomes	27	**T**	
Record keeping	132-134	Tall fescue	151-153
Red fescue	154	Tax deductions	134
Referrals	88-92	Tax records	133
Renovation	172-173	Tax warning	135
Repeat customers	115-118	Telemarketing	93-94, 100-103
Rhizomes	151	Term loans	147
Roots	150	Terracare aerator	27
Rubber stamps	126	Thatch buildup	15
Rust (disease)	177	Tie-downs	37
Ryan Lawnaire 28	28-30	Tillers	150
		Time management	130-132
S		Top dressing	173
Sales, door-to-door	112-114	Trailers	32
Sales, closing	103-104	Trapped gases	15
SALSCO	27	Truck	31-32
Sand	161	Turf management	149-178
SBA loans	146	Turf ryegrass	155
Schedule divider	131-132	Turning radius	48
Scheduling	130-132	Typewriter	124
Seasonal planning	135-136		
Selling attitude	97-98	**U**	
Selling	97-120	Unpaid bills	132
Signature loans	147		
Signs	86-88	**V**	
Snapper	28	Value, building	104-105
Soil Conditioner	38, 59-60		
Soil Barriers	16	**W**	
Soil Ph	161-162	Want, developing	107-108
Soil	160-161	Water runoff	13
Sole proprietorship	141-142	Watering	171-172
Spiking	12	Weeds	174-175
Sprinklers	46-47	Wheel cage	32-33
Spotted Spurge	175		
Spreader	35	**Y**	
St. Augustine	158-159	Yellow pages	66, 128
St. Augustine Decline	159		
Start-up Kit	138, 188		
Start-up costs	19-24		
Stationery	125-126		
Steer manure	173		
Stolons	152		
Suburban pricing	54-57		
Suffocation	14		
Sulfur	165		
Sweeping	50		